FUN AND EASY
Crafting
WITH
Recycled
Materials

60 Cool Projects that Reimagine Paper Rolls,
Egg Cartons, Jars and More!

Kimberly McLeod

CREATOR OF
The Best Ideas for Kids®

PAGE STREET
PUBLISHING CO.

PAGE STREET
PUBLISHING CO.

Copyright © 2019 Kimberly McLeod

First published in 2019 by
Page Street Publishing Co.
27 Congress Street, Suite 1511
Salem, MA 01970
www.pagestreetpublishing.com

Distributed by Macmillan, sales in Canada by The Canadian Manda Group.

24   7

ISBN-13: 978-1-62414-908-5
ISBN-10: 1-62414-908-1

Library of Congress Control Number: 2019940342

Cover and book design by Kylie Alexander for Page Street Publishing Co.
Photography by Kimberly McLeod
Template designs by Ruxandra Serbanoiu

Printed and bound in the United States

Dedicated to
my biggest fan—
my husband—and
to my inspiring and
imaginative kids.

CONTENTS

Introduction 7

CHAPTER ONE
The Basics 8

CHAPTER TWO
Fun Paper Roll Activities 11

Cute Owl 12

Cheerful Butterfly 14

Thankful Turkey 16

3-D Butterfly Bracelet 18

Sparkly Necklace 20

Rainbow Rainstick 22

Backyard Safari Binoculars 24

Paper Roll Printing 26

Easy Flower Stamps 28

Supply Organizer 30

Stacking Challenge 32

Homemade Kaleidoscope 34

CHAPTER THREE
Eggcellent Egg Carton Ideas 39

Fun Snowman 40

Penguin Antarctica Play Scene 42

Rainbow Caterpillar 44

3-D Hot-Air Balloon 46

Beautiful Flowers Card 48

Indoor Mini-Garden 50

Seed Starter Planters 52

Crystal Growing Project 54

CHAPTER FOUR

Nifty Newspaper and Scrap Paper Projects   57

Fun Paper Plate Snail   58
Three-Season Scrap Paper Trees   60
Letter Initial Canvas Art   62
Adorable Torn-Paper Cactus   64
Newspaper Pirate Hat   66
Easy Monkey Face   68
Newspaper Tropical Wreath   70

CHAPTER FIVE

Cool Cardboard Creations   73

Rainbow Turtle Puzzle   74
Rainbow and Cloud with Pop Tabs   76
Build Your Own Marble Maze   78
Silly Tissue Box Monster   80
Rainbow Jellyfish   82
Shoebox Aquarium   84
Shoebox Winter Diorama   86
Cereal Box Farm Puppet Theater   88
Awesome Cardboard Castle   91
Simple Princess Crown   94
Cool Superhero Mask   96
Cookie-Cutter Christmas Ornaments   98

CHAPTER SIX

Easy Ice Pop Stick Projects   101

Simple Sailboat   102
Fun Airplane   104
Easy Paper Fan   106
Weather Puzzle   108
Boredom Buster Jar   110
Personalized Trinket Box   112
Magnet Frame   114
Colorful Easter Basket   116

CHAPTER SEVEN

Awesome Jars, Bottles and More   119

Mason Jar Spring Globe   120
Smell Jar Game   122
Dinosaur Terrarium   124
Tissue Paper Jar Luminaire   126
Silly Face Jars   128
Bottle Maracas   130
Spring Discovery Bottle   132
Milk Carton Bird Feeder   134
Bottle Cap Bees   136
Pouch Bottle Cap Flower   138
Rainbow Bottle Cap Paint Palette   140
Margarine Container Birthday Cake   142
Plastic Container Suncatcher   144

Acknowledgments   146
About the Author   147
Templates   149
Index   157

A Note to Parents

This book was written for kids; however, all activities should be supervised by an adult. There are some projects that require adult assistance, such as projects needing a craft knife or borax. I have noted these at the beginning of the project and during the steps involved. Some projects require hot glue. For younger kids, please provide assistance for these steps. For older kids who can properly use a glue gun, please supervise during these steps. And a friendly reminder to always read and follow all of the tool and product manufacturers' instructions.

INTRODUCTION

Welcome to *Fun and Easy Crafting with Recycled Materials*! If you're looking for easy and fun crafts, you've picked up the right book. With 60 cool projects, this book has crafts and activities for kids of all ages! A range of projects is included, from larger, challenging projects like a cardboard castle (page 91) to quick and easy projects like paper fans (page 106). This book is filled with ideas that will take everyday items that are set for the trash and turn them into new, colorful and fun creations. There is surely something here for everyone!

I'm Kim, the creator behind The Best Ideas for Kids®. My website is filled with easy crafts and activities for kids. Some of our most-loved projects are recycled craft projects, such as reimagining paper rolls as new creations like Christmas ornaments or Halloween decorations. Many of our community members have asked for more recycled project ideas, so I created this book.

For this book, my kids inspired me to take everyday recycled items beyond what I ever thought was possible. In our house, a box has become an airplane, and a piece of cardboard has been transformed into a sword and shield. I hope this book takes you beyond the projects included here to reimagine your everyday items that are set for the recycling bin. You can create *anything* out of *anything* using your imagination. I even surprised my own family with how some of these items were transformed into new things (like the Margarine Container Birthday Cake [page 142]).

Each project has a **TRY THIS!** section to help you take things further with the recycled item or idea. For example, you can make the Bottle Cap Bees on page 136, but can you also try making other bugs out of bottle caps? Save up the recycled materials, and then see what else you can make with them. Don't be discouraged if your end result doesn't look like what's in this book. Every creation is unique, and I hope you enjoy the process of building and creating more than anything.

Happy crafting!

Kim ♡

For even more fun ideas, visit us at thebestideasforkids.com.

CHAPTER ONE

The Basics

There are just a few things to consider before diving into these projects. If you have any questions or problems, please ask an adult.

Items to Save

Here are all of the recycled items to collect for these projects, but don't let this list limit your imagination! Save other things you think you can possibly use to create art or projects! Get your whole family involved in collecting items so you have lots to choose from.

- Cardboard: Break down cardboard for storing. Shipping boxes are great for larger projects; whereas cereal boxes, shoeboxes and snack boxes can be used for smaller projects.

- Jars

- Bottle caps, pouch caps and pop tabs: Some communities and schools collect pop tabs for charities, so be sure to hold on to those to donate, too!

- Ice pop sticks

- Egg cartons

- Plastic containers: Fruit containers work great!

- Paper rolls

- Brown paper bags

- Rubber bands

- Newspaper or colorful magazine pages
- Scrap paper: These can be leftover papers from other craft projects or colorful magazine pages you can cut out.
- Plastic bottles
- Tissue boxes
- Milk or juice cartons
- Bubble wrap
- Tissue paper

Crafting Safety

HOT GLUE

I like to use hot glue for projects that are tougher to glue together or need to be sturdy (like the Colorful Easter Basket [page 116] or the Awesome Cardboard Castle [page 91]). Always be careful when using a hot glue gun and have a parent assist with these steps.

As an alternative, for a lot of projects, I use a nontoxic extra-strong glue for gluing pom-poms, buttons and more. You can find this type of glue at any craft store or craft section of a big box store.

ACRYLIC PAINT

Acrylic paint is my favorite paint for crafts you want to keep. The paint goes on better (fewer coats needed) and is more durable. Be mindful that acrylic paint can stain surfaces and clothes. When painting, wear a paint smock and protect your surfaces. Alternatively, you can use washable paint.

CARDBOARD

Cutting cardboard can be difficult with kid's scissors. Ask a parent for help with these steps if you are having difficulty.

CRAFT KNIFE

Some projects require the use of a craft knife. Get an adult to assist with these steps.

CHAPTER TWO

Fun Paper Roll Activities

How many different things can you create out of one simple paper roll? From a Homemade Kaleidoscope (page 34) to a 3-D Butterfly Bracelet (page 18), you can create just about anything! You can even stack them, paint them or roll them. With these projects, you'll transform an everyday item into something completely new!

STORING TIP: Keep paper rolls stored in a box so they do not get bent or flattened.

Cute Owl

These owls are a hoot to make! Using paper rolls, newspaper and cardboard, you can create a whole bunch of these adorable friends. Create unique designs by painting the whole paper roll a color, adding googly eyes or even craft feathers.

MATERIALS

Paint

Paintbrush

Newspaper

Paper roll

Scissors

Extra-strong glue

Pencil

White and orange cardstock

Black marker

Cardboard

TRY THIS!

What other animals can you make out of a paper roll? Try making a bear or a monkey.

DIRECTIONS

Decide what color you want the front of your owl to be and paint a piece of newspaper that color.

For the owl's ears, bend in the top portion of the paper roll on each side. Bend just a little bit from the top or the paper roll may fold in too much.

Cut out an oval shape from your newspaper and glue it to the front of the paper roll. Trim off the bottom if needed.

For the eyes, trace 2 circles using the end of a small glue stick or another similar circle shape on the white cardstock. Cut them out. Glue the eyes to the top of the paper roll, and then add a small dot with the black marker.

For the beak, fold over a small piece of orange cardstock. Draw a small triangle shape right at the fold you made, and then cut it out. Glue this under the eyes.

For the wings, draw a wing shape on a piece of cardboard and cut it out. Then use that shape to draw another one and cut that out as well. Glue the wings on both sides of the owl.

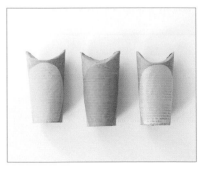

Cheerful Butterfly

These butterflies are so colorful that you will love making them! The wings are easy to make with the template provided in the back of the book (page 151). Have fun decorating the wings however you'd like! You can use pom-poms, buttons or even just color on your own designs.

MATERIALS

Paper roll

Paint

Paintbrush

Colored cardstock or construction paper

Butterfly wing template (page 151)

Pencil

Scissors

Extra-strong glue

6 colored buttons

1 pipe cleaner

2 small pom-poms

Googly eyes

Black marker

DIRECTIONS

Paint the paper roll a color of your choice and let it dry. You may need to paint a few coats for lighter colors.

For the wings, fold a piece of cardstock in half. Trace the template on page 151 onto the cardstock at the fold you made. Cut out the wings.

Glue colored buttons to the butterfly wings.

To make the antennae, bend the pipe cleaner into the shape of a "V". Curl the tips of the "V" down. Glue 2 small pom-poms to the tips.

Glue the antennae to the inside top of the paper roll. Glue the googly eyes near the top of the paper roll and draw a mouth with the black marker. Glue the wings to the back of the paper roll.

TRY THIS! Use the butterfly wings to make another butterfly craft. Can you make a bottle butterfly?

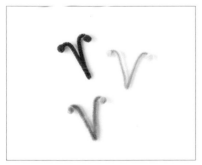

Thankful Turkey

Making a Thankful Turkey is a great way to reflect on the things that you are thankful for in your life. These turkeys can be used for table decoration during Thanksgiving or even just to decorate around your home.

MATERIALS

Paper roll

Brown acrylic paint

Paintbrush

Turkey feather template
(page 151)

Pencil

Red, yellow and orange
cardstock or construction
paper

Scissors

Black marker

Glue

Googly eyes

DIRECTIONS

Paint the paper roll brown and let it dry. You may need a few coats to fully cover the paper roll.

For the feathers, trace the template on page 151 on the cardstock until you have at least 5 feathers. Then cut them out. With the black marker, write on each feather the things you are thankful for.

Glue 2 googly eyes near the top of the paper roll.

For the beak, fold over a small piece of orange cardstock. Draw a small triangle shape right at the fold you made, then cut it out. Glue this under the eyes.

Draw the feet on cardstock by making a triangle shape and then drawing 3 toes at the base of the triangle. Cut out the feet and glue them to the turkey.

Glue the feathers to the back of the turkey.

 TRY THIS! Make a matching turkey from a brown paper bag.

3-D Butterfly Bracelet

These 3-D Butterfly Bracelets are a lot of fun to make and wear!
They are also so quick and easy to make that you'll want to make one
for all of your friends!

MATERIALS

Paper roll

Metallic acrylic paint

Paintbrush

Scissors

Butterfly template (page 151)

Pencil

Colored cardstock

Ruler

Craft gems

Extra-strong glue

Markers (optional)

DIRECTIONS

Paint the paper roll a color of your choice and let it dry. Metallic acrylic paints are perfect for this craft since they will make the bracelet look more like real jewelry.

Cut the paper roll to the size you'd like your bracelet to be. Then make a vertical cut on the paper roll piece so that you can fit the roll over your wrist.

To make the butterfly, trace the template on page 151 on a piece of colored cardstock. Cut out the butterfly. To create the 3-D effect, make 2 folds on the inside of the butterfly with the ruler (see photo for fold placement). This will make the butterfly wings stand up while the center piece is flat for gluing.

Glue craft gems to your butterfly. You can also color and decorate the wings with markers.

Glue the butterfly on top of your paper roll.

TRY THIS! Make other bracelet styles from paper rolls. Add a flower or just decorate the paper roll with craft gems or paint.

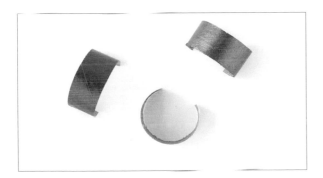

Sparkly Necklace

Making jewelry is a fun craft, but the best part is you can wear it when you're done! Create your own paper roll necklace in any color you'd like, and then add some sparkle with a few craft gems.

MATERIALS

Several paper rolls

Acrylic paint

Paintbrush

Scissors

Extra-strong glue

Craft gems

DIRECTIONS

Paint the paper rolls in the colors you want your necklace to be. You may need a few coats to fully cover the paper rolls.

Cut the paper rolls into equal-sized pieces. Cut 3 larger pieces for the bottom of the necklace.

Paint the inside of the pieces the same color as the outside. You can also paint the inside before cutting them, but it is easier to paint when they have been cut into smaller pieces.

To assemble the necklace, cut a slit into 1 side of 1 of the bigger bottom pieces. This is so you can loop it around another piece. Then glue it around another piece. Glue the 3 bigger paper roll pieces together following this process. Add a gem to the middle one for design.

Continue to add the smaller paper roll pieces until you are happy with the size of your necklace. Glue any other craft gems or decorations to your necklace, if you'd like.

TRY THIS! Make some matching paper roll bracelets.

Rainbow Rainstick

Make the pitter-patter sound of the rain with some sticks, rice and a paper towel roll. These are so easy to put together, and you'll love the soothing sound they make. Create a whole rainbow set or just make one for yourself!

MATERIALS

Paper towel roll

Acrylic paint

Paintbrush

Masking tape

Sticks

⅓ cup (66 g) or more uncooked rice

Paper bag

Scissors

2 rubber bands

Washi tape and stickers, for decorating (optional)

DIRECTIONS

Paint the paper towel roll the color of your choice. You may need a few coats to fully cover the paper roll.

Once the paint is dry, tape the bottom of the paper roll with the masking tape.

Fill the paper towel roll with sticks. Tightly compact the sticks and add as many different shapes and sizes as you can. When the rice falls through the sticks, you want them to bounce around to make the sound of rain.

Pour the rice into the paper roll. You can experiment with more or less rice to hear the difference it makes. Seal the open end of the roll with masking tape.

Cut 2 small square pieces from the paper bag. Cover 1 end of the roll with a square and wrap the rubber band around it to hold it in place. Repeat on the other end. You can also decorate your rainsticks with washi tape, stickers or other embellishments to bring them to life.

Gently tip the rainstick back and forth to hear the pitter-patter sound of rain falling!

TRY THIS! Add some small beans or pebbles instead to see if it makes a different sound. Or make a longer rainstick with a wrapping-paper tube.

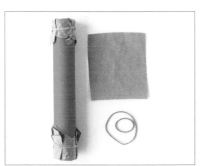
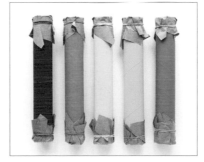
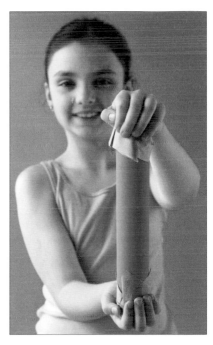

Backyard Safari Binoculars

Go out exploring on a backyard safari with your own homemade binoculars. Create a scavenger hunt to see how many items you can find! See how many different sticks, rocks, leaves and flowers you can find on your adventure!

MATERIALS

2 paper rolls

Paint

Paintbrush

Yarn, washi tape or colored tape, for decorating (optional)

Cardboard

Scissors

Tape

Extra-strong glue

Single-hole puncher

Twine or string

 **TRY THIS!**

Make other pretend safari supplies, such as a magnifying glass out of cardboard and a recycled plastic sheet.

DIRECTIONS

Paint 2 paper rolls the color you'd like your binoculars to be. You may need a few coats to fully cover the rolls.

Decorate your binoculars however you'd like! Add yarn, washi tape, colored tape or even some paint designs. Add some colored yellow tape to the ends to make it look like binoculars. You can also paint this on instead.

Cut out a rectangular piece of cardboard (approximately 2 inches wide by 2.5 inches long [5 x 6.25 cm]). Fold it over so that it forms a rectangular box. Tape the rectangular box together and then glue it in-between both paper rolls. (You can also simply glue the 2 paper rolls together lengthwise.)

Punch a hole on each side of the binoculars where the twine will hang. Cut a piece of twine that will fit around your neck. Tie the twine through the hole punches on the sides of the binoculars.

Create your own scavenger hunt, and then go out exploring on a backyard safari!

Paper Roll Printing

Paper rolls can be used for paint printing. Add foam shapes or bubble wrap and then roll out your designs. You can even create your own wrapping paper by printing on large rolls of paper.

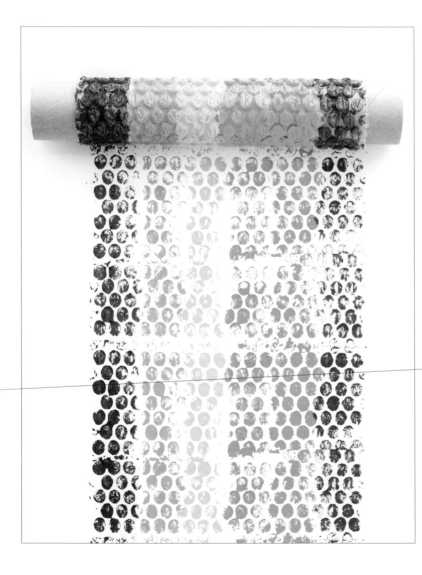

MATERIALS

Bubble wrap

Scissors

2 paper towel rolls

Glue

Paint

Paintbrush

Paper

Foam shapes

TRY THIS!

Try out other designs by cutting out your own foam shapes and see what print designs they make.

DIRECTIONS

To make the rainbow bubble wrap print, cut a piece of bubble wrap that will fit around the paper towel roll. Glue the bubble wrap around the roll, leaving some space on each side where you can place your hands for rolling.

Add paint to the bubble wrap. If you'd like to make a rainbow, measure out how many bubbles you'll need to paint for each color.

Once your roller is filled with paint, roll it out on the paper to see the design! Keep adding extra paint as needed if you want to keep rolling.

To print with foam shapes, glue the shapes to the other paper towel roll. Paint the shapes and then print the design by rolling on paper. If you add thicker foam pieces, you can roll the whole paper roll in paint instead.

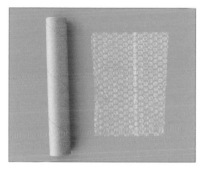

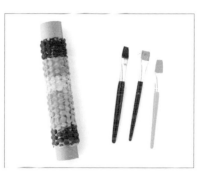

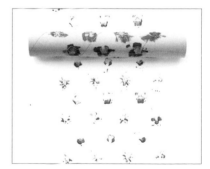

Easy Flower Stamps

Turn paper rolls into flower stamps by cutting out some flower designs on the top. Then add some paint to a paper plate or dish and stamp away!

MATERIALS

Several paper rolls

Scissors

Rubber band

Paint

Paper plates

White cardstock

Green pipe cleaners

Extra-strong glue

Buttons

 TRY THIS!

What other shapes can you make from a paper roll? Can you make a square or use the round shape to print other designs?

DIRECTIONS

To make the pink flower, cut 10 equally spaced slits around the top of the paper roll where the petals will be. Cut around these areas to make them round like a petal. Then gently press the petals down.

To make the purple flower, cut lots of small slits into the top of the paper roll. Then gently press all of the slit pieces down.

To make the orange flower, fold the paper roll in half. Use a rubber band to hold it in place.

Pour the paint onto paper plates or a dish. Then dip the ends of the paper rolls into the paint and stamp onto the cardstock to make your flowers!

Make a flower art piece by gluing green pipe cleaners for the stems. You can also draw a stem and leaf on or use paper. To make a leaf, fold over a smaller piece of pipe cleaner and glue this down. Glue a button inside each flower print.

Supply Organizer

Brighten up your desk with these colorful paper roll organizers!
Make small ones or large ones, and place all of your favorite
craft supplies in these simple organizers!

MATERIALS

Ruler

Cardboard

Scissors

3–5 paper rolls

Paint

Paintbrush

Painting tape (optional)

Hot glue gun and hot-melt
glue sticks

DIRECTIONS

For the base of the organizer, decide how many pencil holders you want. Measure with the ruler and then cut out a cardboard rectangle that will be big enough for your holders.

Paint the paper rolls and the cardboard base. To paint stripes or diagonals, first paint the paper roll with one lighter color, like orange or light blue. Allow this paint to dry. Then add painting tape to create your design. Paint the second color on top. Once dry, carefully peel off the painting tape.

Have an adult help to hot glue the paper rolls to the cardboard base.

Add your supplies to your holders! These are great for storing pencils and markers.

TRY THIS! Turn the paper roll organizer into a caterpillar paper roll organizer. Add eyes, a mouth and antennae to the first paper roll.

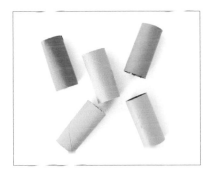

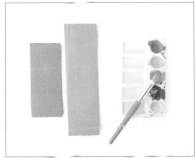

Stacking Challenge

How high can you stack a set of paper rolls before your structure falls over? This is an easy STEM challenge you can make on your own. With just paper rolls and cardboard, you can create so many different designs. Then challenge your friends to see who can build the tallest structure!

MATERIALS

10 or more paper rolls

Cardboard

Paint

Paintbrush

Scissors

Ruler

DIRECTIONS

Paint the paper rolls and cardboard in different bright colors to make the pieces fun and colorful. You may need a few coats to fully cover the paper rolls.

Cut at least 5 strips of cardboard in different sizes ranging from 3 inches (7.6 cm) to over 6 inches (15 cm).

Cut each paper roll in half to make 2 smaller rolls. Cut 2 slit marks on each side of the paper roll, both at the top and bottom. This is where the cardboard strips will fit in. Make sure to test that the cardboard pieces will fit and if not, cut a little more out of the paper rolls.

See how many paper rolls you can stack! Start a base layer of 2 or more paper rolls. Add a cardboard piece. Then add a paper roll and keep stacking. How many can you add before your whole structure topples over? See who can build the highest structure!

TRY THIS! What other stacking methods can you create with cardboard and paper rolls? Try making 4 slits on the top and bottom in a paper roll and then stack them on top of each other.

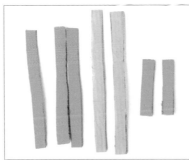
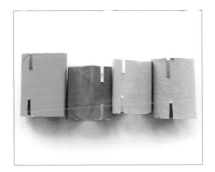

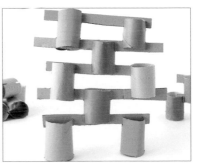

Homemade Kaleidoscope

Create your own kaleidoscope with a paper towel roll, mirrored sheet cardstock (which you can find at craft stores) and beads. Then, point it toward the light to see the magic!

MATERIALS

Paper towel roll

Plastic container sheet (cut from a fruit container or other plastic packaging)

Permanent marker

Scissors

Mirrored sheet of cardstock or foil board sheet

Ruler

Clear tape

Paint

Paintbrush

Colored translucent beads

Colored cardstock

Colored tape or stickers, for decorating (optional)

DIRECTIONS

Use the paper towel roll to help you trace 2 circles on the clear plastic sheet. One circle will need to fit inside the paper roll and the other has to fit on the edge of one end of the paper roll. Cut out the plastic circles.

Measure a piece of the mirror sheet so that it is slightly shorter than the length of your paper roll. You want to be able to form this sheet into a triangle that's inserted into the paper roll. For a paper towel roll, the size of the mirror sheet will be approximately 4.6 inches (11.7 cm) wide by 10.5 inches (26.7 cm) tall.

Fold the mirror sheet to form a long triangle, with the mirror side facing inside the triangle. Tape it together to hold it in this shape.

Paint the paper roll and let it dry. You may need a few coats to fully cover the paper roll.

Insert the mirror sheet all the way into the paper roll. It should be flush with one end, and the other end should have enough space to fit your beads.

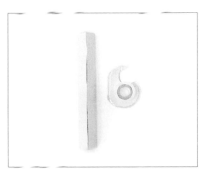

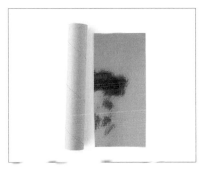
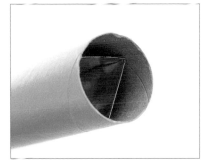

(continued)

Homemade Kaleidoscope (continued)

Add 1 plastic circle inside the paper roll on the side where there is space to fit your beads. Tape it to the paper towel roll, if needed.

Add the beads on top of the inside plastic circle. Try not to overpack the beads or they will not be able to move around when you turn the kaleidoscope.

Tape the remaining plastic circle on top of the beads.

On the opposite end, add a circular piece of cardstock with a peephole in the center. Trace around the paper roll on the cardstock to make your circle shape and cut it out. You can make the peephole by gently folding the paper over to create a slit mark with your scissors. Then cut out a circle shape from the center.

Decorate your kaleidoscope with some colored tape, stickers or cardstock. Then shine your kaleidoscope into some light and turn it around to see the magic!

TRY THIS! Try different materials inside your kaleidoscope, such as confetti, to see the difference it makes. A paper towel roll is the perfect size for this project, but you can also experiment with making a smaller or larger one!

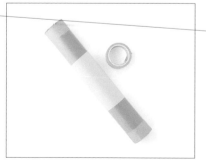

CHAPTER THREE

Eggcellent Egg Carton Ideas

Egg cartons can be used in so many ways! You can use them as seed starters for your garden (page 52), turn them into fun hot-air balloons (page 46) or even make your very own Penguin Antarctica Play Scene (page 42)!

STORING TIP: Stack egg cartons on top of each other to save space.

👍 Fun Snowman

Create a playful snowman from egg cartons. This is an easy winter or Christmas craft. Add personality to your snowman by adding a scarf, pipe-cleaner arms or a homemade hat.

MATERIALS

Egg carton

Scissors

White acrylic paint

Paintbrush

Extra-strong glue

1 pipe cleaner

Small pom-poms in the color you'd like to make your ear muffs

1 sheet of orange cardstock or construction paper

Black marker

2 black buttons

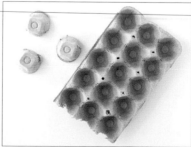

DIRECTIONS

Cut out 3 egg cups from the egg carton.

Paint the cups white. Allow them to fully dry. You may need a few coats to fully cover the cups.

To make the body, cut out 2 small strips (approximately 1 inch wide by 3.5 inches long [2.5 x 8.75 cm]) from the egg carton lid. Fold each into a cube. Glue them to the tops of 2 of the egg cups. This will allow your other egg cups to sit slightly higher on top of each other. You can also scrunch some scrap paper into a ball and then glue it to the top of the 2 cups.

Glue 1 of the egg cups with the cardboard on top of the other one. Then glue your final egg cup (without the egg carton piece spacer) on top of this.

To make the earmuffs, cut a small piece of pipe cleaner and bend it so it fits on top of the snowman's head. Glue it to the top of the head. Glue the pom-poms on each side of the pipe cleaner to make it look like earmuffs.

Draw a carrot nose on the orange cardstock and then cut it out. You can make the nose a triangle or make it a little more rounded. Glue the nose to the snowman's face. Then draw the eyes and mouth with a black marker.

Glue the black buttons on the middle and bottom egg cups.

TRY THIS! Can you make a Christmas tree out of egg cartons?

Penguin Antarctica Play Scene

Create your own penguin play scene with some egg carton penguins, packaging foam, cotton balls and blue paper for water. Then have fun playing with these egg carton penguins! You can make one or a whole colony.

MATERIALS

Egg carton

Scissors

Black and white acrylic paint

Paintbrush

White pipe cleaner

Extra-strong glue

2 small white pom-poms

Sheet of orange cardstock or construction paper

Googly eyes

2 small orange pom-poms

Cotton balls

Packaging foam

Blue paper

DIRECTIONS

Cut out 2 egg cups from the egg carton.

Paint the egg cups black. Allow them to fully dry. You may need a few coats to fully cover the cups.

Paint a white belly on 1 of the egg cups. This will be the penguin's body. You may need a few coats of the white paint.

To make the earmuffs, cut a small piece of pipe cleaner and bend it so it fits on top of the head. Glue to the penguin head carton piece.

Glue the white pom-poms on each side of the pipe cleaner to make it look like earmuffs.

To make the penguin's beak, fold a small piece of cardstock over and cut out a triangle at the fold. Glue it to the penguin's head.

Glue 2 googly eyes above the beak. Glue 2 small orange pom-poms to the body for feet.

To put the body together, cut out 1 small strip from the egg carton lid. Fold it into a square. Glue it to the top of the body cup. This will allow the head to sit slightly higher on top of the body. You can also scrunch some scrap paper into a ball and glue it to the top of the body cup.

Glue the head to the body. Now you have your finished egg carton penguin.

Add cotton balls, packaging foam and blue paper on a table to create your Antarctica play scene!

 TRY THIS! Can you make a rain forest play scene or a farm scene from egg cartons and other recycled materials?

Rainbow Caterpillar

You can turn egg cartons into all sorts of insects and animals. This rainbow caterpillar is my favorite egg carton craft. If you're looking for a quick and simple craft to make, this is the one!

MATERIALS

Egg carton

Scissors

White, red, orange, yellow, green, blue and purple acrylic paint

Paintbrush

Black pipe cleaner

Pencil

Glue

Googly eyes

Black marker

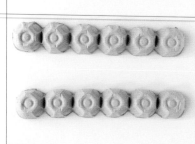

DIRECTIONS

Cut off the egg carton top. Cut along the middle of the egg carton to split the egg carton into 2 pieces. Each piece should have 6 cups.

Paint 1 egg carton piece white. Once it is fully dry, paint each cup a different color for a rainbow effect.

Cut 2 small pieces of black pipe cleaner. Curl the tops to form antennae. With the pencil, poke a small hole for each antenna at the top of the caterpillar's head, and then gently push the pipe cleaners inside. You can also glue them to make sure they stay in place.

Glue 2 small googly eyes to the caterpillar's head.

Use the black marker to draw on a smile, and your rainbow caterpillar is done! You can use other colors or make green caterpillars too!

TRY THIS! Make the whole butterfly lifecycle with egg cartons. Create an egg, caterpillar, chrysalis and butterfly.

3-D Hot-Air Balloon

Go up, up and away with these colorful egg carton hot-air balloons! These make beautiful summer window decorations, and you can even add a string to them and hang them from a ceiling.

MATERIALS

Egg carton

Scissors

Brown paint, for decorating (optional)

Paintbrush, for decorating (optional)

Hot-air balloon template (page 155)

Pencil

6 sheets of colored cardstock (different colors for a rainbow effect)

Extra-strong glue

Twine

Hot glue gun and hot-melt glue sticks

Tape, for hanging (optional)

DIRECTIONS

Cut out 1 egg cup from the egg carton. Paint the cup brown or leave it as it is.

To make the balloon, trace the template on page 155 onto 6 different colored cardstock sheets. Create your own color combinations or make a rainbow! Cut each one out.

Fold the balloon pieces in the center. Glue 3 of the pieces together, side by side. Then separately, glue the remaining 3 pieces together side by side. You should now have 2 balloon top pieces.

Cut 2 small pieces of twine approximately 3 inches (7.5 cm) long. Glue them to the bottom center of one of your hot-air balloon pieces, making sure you have at least 2 inches (5 cm) hanging from the bottom of the piece. If you want to hang your hot-air balloon, you'll need to glue another string to the top for hanging.

Glue the 2 hot-air balloon pieces together. Note: If you want to tape the balloon to a window, leave 1 side of each hot-air balloon piece unglued so you can press the balloon flat against the window.

Have and adult help hot glue 1 twine piece to each side of the inside of the egg cup. Tape the hot-air balloons to a window or hang them from the ceiling. You can also add a small photo of yourself inside the egg carton.

 TRY THIS! Use the hot-air balloon template to create your own summer art scene. Add other recycled materials to bring it to life!

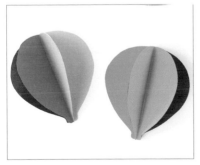

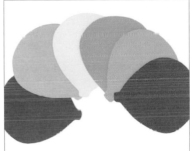

Beautiful Flowers Card

Surprise your mom or grandma with this beautiful handmade egg carton flower card. They'll be delighted to receive this for their birthday or Mother's Day!

MATERIALS

Egg carton

Scissors

Paint

Paintbrush

Extra-strong glue

3 buttons

White and green cardstock

Green pipe cleaners

Ribbon

DIRECTIONS

Cut out 6 egg carton cups in order to make 3 flowers.

Trim around 3 of the cups to make 4 petals.

With the remaining cups, cut out 4 small petals for each flower cup. These will be added to the egg cups to make more petals.

Paint the flower egg cups and petals in different shades if you'd like. Allow them to fully dry.

Glue the petals to the outside of the flower cups, between the petals.

Glue a button inside each flower.

To make the card, fold the white cardstock in the center and trim to form the size of a card. Glue the 3 flowers to the top of the card.

Cut 3 pipe cleaners to fit under your flowers. Glue them to the card.

Cut out a few leaves from the green cardstock and glue to the card. Glue a ribbon bow on top of the stems.

TRY THIS! Turn this into wall art by gluing egg carton flowers to some cardstock and then framing it.

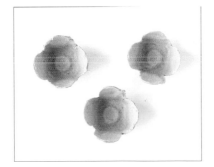

Indoor Mini-Garden

Create your own indoor garden with paper, ice pop sticks and an egg carton!
Make different kinds of flowers on your own or use the templates in this book
to trace the designs. Brighten up your room or family kitchen with
your own garden that will bloom year-round!

MATERIALS

18-count egg carton*

Scissors

Green paint

Paintbrush

10 ice pop sticks

Mini-garden templates
(page 151)

Pencil

Pink, purple, yellow, red and
green cardstock

Extra-strong glue

Several small buttons

*Note: If you don't have an
18-count egg carton, which will
give you 2 rows of flowers, you
can use a 12-count carton and do
1 row of flowers instead.*

DIRECTIONS

Cut off the top of the egg carton. Paint the egg carton green. You may need a few coats to fully cover the carton. Let it dry. Paint the sticks green. Let them dry.

To make the flowers, trace the templates on page 151 on the cardstock. Cut out the flowers. Glue the buttons to the center of the 5-petal flowers. Glue the flowers to the top of the sticks.

Draw some leaves on the green cardstock and cut them out. Glue the leaves to each flower.

With the pencil, poke small holes at the top of each egg carton cone. Push the flowers into the holes. If they don't stand up on their own, use some glue to keep them in place.

TRY THIS! Make a vegetable garden instead! Make paper tomatoes, carrots and lettuce to add to your egg carton garden.

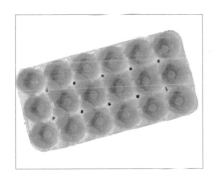
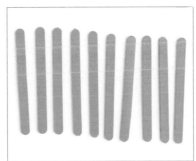

Seed Starter Planters

Grow your vegetable seedlings with these egg carton seed starters!
Get a green thumb this summer and enjoy your own vegetables
straight from the garden!

MATERIALS

Egg carton

Scissors

Potting soil

2-3 seeds per egg cup

Plastic tray

Water

TRY THIS!

Make garden markers with
ice pop sticks. Write the plant
names on the sticks with a
permanent marker.

✔ RECYCLING TIP!

Compostable materials can
be placed in green bins
(if your community accepts
them). You can also create
your own compost and turn
this into dirt you can use to
plant your own garden.

DIRECTIONS

Cut off the top of the egg carton.

Check your seed package for planting directions. Not all vegetables need to be started indoors (see packaging for details on timing).

Place some moistened soil inside the egg cups.

Add 2 to 3 seeds to each egg cup. Add a small layer of soil on top of the seeds.

Place the egg carton on the plastic tray. Add a little bit of water to the bottom of the tray so that the egg carton can soak it up.

Lightly water the egg cups each day.

According to the type of seed, you may start to see germination within 7 to 10 days. Once leaves start to form, trim down any extra plants in each egg cup so that you have only 1 plant per cup.

Before planting outdoors you'll need to acclimate your seedlings. Put them outdoors when the temperature is mild and bring the plants indoors at night. Gradually increase the time you leave them outdoors during the day. After 7 to 10 days, your plants should be ready to transfer.

Once you are ready to plant outdoors, gently squeeze the carton a few times from all sides to loosen the dirt. Then carefully remove both the dirt and the plant together. Do not pull the plant out by the stem. If you're still having trouble, soak the egg carton in water until it is very soft. You should now be able to carefully peel the egg carton away from the roots of the plant to allow you to plant outdoors.

Recycle the egg carton by cutting it into smaller pieces, and then place it in your compost!

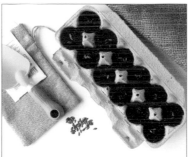

ADULT ASSISTANCE REQUIRED

Crystal Growing Project

Grow your own crystals with this recycled science experiment! You'll be amazed that egg cartons can look like geodes. Make different colors to add to your mock-geode collection!

MATERIALS

Egg carton

Scissors

Water

Glass Mason jar

Safety goggles

Gloves

6 tbsp (84 g) borax

Spoon

Food coloring

Tongs

Paper towels

Magnifying glass

TRY THIS!

Instead of egg cartons, try growing crystals inside egg shells.

DIRECTIONS

Cut out 1 egg carton cup. If you'd like to make more than 1 geode, multiply the materials by how many egg carton geodes you want to create!

Have an adult boil the water and place 2 cups (480 ml) of boiled water into the Mason jar.

Put on the safety goggles and gloves. Have an adult add the borax to the Mason jar and carefully stir with the spoon. Stir until all of the borax is dissolved.

Add a few drops of food coloring to the mixture and stir.

Using tongs, place 1 egg cup into the jar so it is positioned with the flat bottom touching the bottom of the jar. (This will allow the crystals to grow mostly inside the cup.)

Leave the jar for 24 hours, which is when you should see crystals starting to form.

After 24 hours, remove the cup from the jar with the tongs and let the cup dry on the paper towels.

Get a magnifying glass and examine the crystals up close!

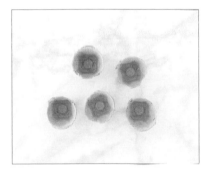

CHAPTER FOUR

Nifty Newspaper and Scrap Paper Projects

Don't throw out those little scraps of paper! You can save these little pieces, cut them up and make beautiful torn-paper arts and crafts! Newspaper can be painted and turned into new creations too—like a Newspaper Tropical Wreath (page 70) or an Easy Monkey Face (page 68)!

STORING TIP: Keep scrap paper organized by color to save time when crafting.

Fun Paper Plate Snail

You can craft at a snail's pace to make this scrap paper plate snail. Grab all those extra scraps of paper and make small squares to use in this simple snail craft. Making a snail's head has never been easier with the template included in this book!

MATERIALS

Scrap paper in different colors

Scissors

Glue

Small paper plate

Snail template (page 155)

Pencil

Yellow cardstock or construction paper

Googly eyes

Black marker

DIRECTIONS

Gather the scrap paper colors you want to use for the snail. Cut the scrap paper into small square pieces.

Glue the square pieces to the paper plate starting at the edge and working your way around in a spiral pattern. Leave a space at the beginning for where the snail's head will go. You can make a pattern with your colors or mix them up!

To make the snail's head, trace the template on page 155 on the yellow cardstock and cut it out.

Glue 2 googly eyes to the tentacles of the snail. Draw a smiley face with the black marker.

Glue the snail's head to the back of the paper plate.

TRY THIS! Can you make other recycled snails? Try other materials for the shell, like some rolled-up newspaper!

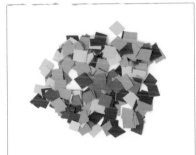
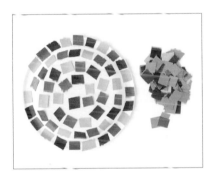

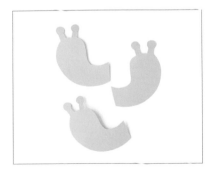
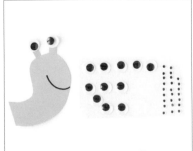

Three-Season Scrap Paper Trees

Turn some old magazine pages into seasonal paper trees! Make spring, summer and fall trees. You can even make a winter tree on black paper by drawing a bare tree on cardboard and then adding white paper scraps for snow.

MATERIALS

Old magazines

Scissors

Cardboard

3 pieces of white cardstock

Glue

Small dish

Paintbrush

✔ RECYCLING TIP!

Flatten boxes and follow your town's rules for what items can go in blue bins.

DIRECTIONS

Flip through old magazines and find pages with blocks of color. For your spring tree, collect different light green colors and a few tones of light pink. For your summer tree, collect darker greens and bright greens. For your fall tree, collect yellow, orange and red.

Cut out these blocks of color and cut them into small square pieces.

Cut out the trunks of the trees from the cardboard to fit approximately half the size of your paper. Glue them to the cardstock.

To create the treetops, squeeze some glue into the dish and then paint the glue onto the area above the trunks. Place your scrap pieces down. Keep filling the trees until you are happy with the way they look!

TRY THIS! If you want a more photo-realistic tree, search for tree and grass photographs in the magazines!

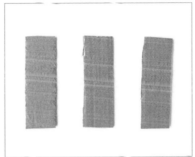

Letter Initial Canvas Art

Hang up a scrap paper initial canvas of your name in your room! You can customize it with colors to match your room, too. You can even spell out your whole name.

MATERIALS

Small canvas

Paint

Paintbrush

Pencil

Scrap paper in different colors

Glue

Small dish (optional)

✔ RECYCLING TIP!

When buying products, choose products made of recycled materials like recycled cardboard.

DIRECTIONS

Paint the canvas the color you'd like for the background. Allow it to fully dry.

With the pencil, gently sketch out the letter you want to make.

Tear the scrap paper into small pieces you can glue down. Choose bright colors to include in the initial.

Layer your scrap paper into the area of the letter. Mix up the colors as you go. Use a paintbrush to brush on the glue and then place the scrap pieces down. You can place some glue into a dish and then paint the glue onto the canvas.

Try to choose pieces with flat edges for the outside of the initial, which will help form the letter. Keep adding pieces until the whole letter is filled in. Repeat for any other letters you wish to create.

TRY THIS! Instead of a canvas, use cardboard as your base. Use a hole punch to add 2 holes at the top, and thread twine through to hang the letter up.

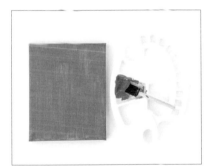

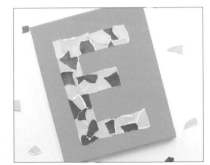

Adorable Torn-Paper Cactus

These cacti will surely put a smile on your face. Make one or all of these friendly cacti to hang up in your room! They are so easy to make with just a few supplies.

MATERIALS

Cardboard

Pencil

Scissors

White, orange, pink and blue acrylic paint

Paintbrush

White cardstock

Glue

White and different shades of green scrap paper

Small dish (optional)

Black marker

Pink tissue paper

DIRECTIONS

Draw and design a flowerpot on the cardboard. Cut it out and paint it. Let it dry.

Paint a design on the flowerpot. Try stripes, curvy lines and/or dots. Let it dry.

Glue the flowerpot to the cardstock.

With the pencil, gently sketch out the design for the cactus following 1 of the 3 different designs shown here. You can also design your own!

Tear the scrap paper into small pieces. Use different colors of green.

Fill in the cactus with the torn paper. Use 1 color or mix and match different parts of the cactus with different colors. Use a paintbrush to brush on the glue and then place the scrap pieces down. You can place some glue into a dish and then paint the glue onto the cardstock.

Add darker colored "V"-shaped torn-paper details on top of the cactus, or use torn white strips.

With the black marker, draw a face. Dip the end of the paintbrush with light-pink paint and add some cheeks.

Cut out some small pieces of pink tissue paper. Wrap them around the bottom of the pencil and dip into some glue. Glue to the top of the cactus for flowers.

 TRY THIS! What other torn-paper art can you make? Try making a torn-paper flower or a torn-paper beach scene.

Newspaper Pirate Hat

Arrr, matey, you can't be a pirate without a pirate hat! Aye, and this pirate hat is the easiest one you'll make. Create a bunch of them so you and your friends can go treasure hunting.

MATERIALS

Newspaper

Scissors

Black paint

Paintbrush

Ruler

Tape or glue

Skull and crossbones template (page 155)

Pencil

White cardstock

TRY THIS!

Make sailor hats by painting the hats white and blue instead of black.

DIRECTIONS

Cut out 1 sheet of newspaper. Paint the whole sheet black. Paint both sides if you want the whole hat to be black. Let it dry.

Place the newspaper vertically (as you would normally hold it upright) on a table. Fold the newspaper in half by folding the top to the bottom of the newspaper.

Take the right and left top corners of the folded side and fold them down to the center. (Measure the center point first with a ruler if needed.)

Take the bottom part of the top sheet of newspaper and fold it up towards the triangle piece.

Flip the hat over.

Fold in a small strip on the left and right side of the hat. Tape or glue the top part of the strip down. This will make the hat smaller and sturdier. If you need the hat to be smaller, fold larger strips here.

Fold the bottom part of the newspaper up.

Turn the hat back over. The newspaper hat is finished! Now you can add the skull and crossbones to the front. Trace the template on page 155 on the white cardstock. Cut it out and glue the skull and crossbones to the front of the hat.

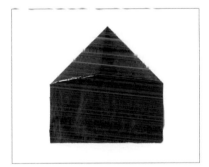

Easy Monkey Face

Did you oooh-oooh-ahhh-ahhh know that you can turn newspaper into a monkey? You can easily make a newspaper monkey face with the templates on page 153. Recycle some newspaper and make your own monkey business!

MATERIALS

5 pieces of newspaper

Black and white acrylic paint plus 2 other colors (a lighter and darker color)

Paintbrush

Monkey face templates (page 153)

Pencil

Scissors

Glue

Black marker

 TRY THIS!

Make a cardboard monkey with a body and a pipe cleaner tail.

DIRECTIONS

Paint 1 large and 1 small newspaper piece in a light color and 2 other pieces in a darker color. The lighter newspaper will be the inside of the monkey face and the ears. The darker sheet will be the head, outside ears and nose. The sheets must be big enough to fit the templates. Let the sheets dry.

For the eyes, paint a small piece of newspaper black. Let it dry.

Turn the newspaper sheets so that the painted sides are face down. Trace the templates (page 153) on the newspaper sheets and cut them out.

Glue the inside of the face to the larger face piece. Glue the inside of the ears to the outer ears. Then glue the ears to the back of the monkey head. Glue the eyes and nose to the monkey face.

With the black marker, draw a mouth coming down from the nose.

Dip the back of the paintbrush handle in the white paint and add a white dot to each eye.

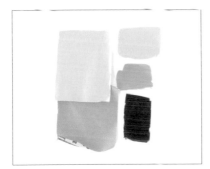  

Newspaper Tropical Wreath

Bring some tropical fun to your home with this vibrant wreath made from newspapers! You can easily make the 3-D flowers with the template on page 149.

MATERIALS

Paper plate

Scissors

3 sheets of newspaper

3 different shades of green paint

Paintbrush

Pencil

Glue

Pink cardstock

Petal template (page 149)

Yellow tissue paper

Ribbon

DIRECTIONS

Cut out the center of the paper plate and set it aside. This will form the base for the wreath.

Paint the sheets of newspaper in the 3 different shades of green. Let them dry.

Place the painted sides of the newspaper sheets face down. Draw 1 leaf on one of the sheets and cut it out. Use this leaf as a template to trace at least 3 leaves on each colored sheet. You should have 9 leaves in total. Cut them out.

Fold each leaf in half, and then cut slits toward the center of the leaf. Angle the cuts towards the bottom of the leaf as shown.

Glue the leaves around the paper plate in a clockwise direction, layering each one on top of the other while alternating colors.

To make the flower, trace the petal template on page 149 on the pink cardstock 5 times. Cut out each of the petals and glue them together to make a flower. Trim off the pointy tip of the petals if needed to glue them together.

Wrap a small square of yellow tissue paper around the bottom of the pencil. Glue the tissue paper piece to the center of the flower. Continue adding tissue paper pieces until you are happy with how the flower looks.

Glue the flower to the wreath. Glue a large ribbon to the back for hanging.

TRY THIS! Make a fall wreath with newspaper leaves.

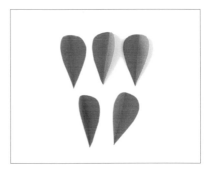

CHAPTER FIVE

Cool Cardboard Creations

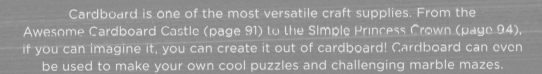

Cardboard is one of the most versatile craft supplies. From the Awesome Cardboard Castle (page 91) to the Simple Princess Crown (page 94), if you can imagine it, you can create it out of cardboard! Cardboard can even be used to make your own cool puzzles and challenging marble mazes.

STORING TIP: Break down and flatten all cardboard to save space.

Rainbow Turtle Puzzle

Making a cardboard puzzle is easier than it looks! There are so many different kinds of puzzles you can make with cardboard! You can make a turtle, but you can also make a rainbow, fish, sun and more!

MATERIALS

Cardboard

Scissors

Pencil

Craft knife

Extra-strong glue

Acrylic paint

Paintbrush

Bubble wrap

DIRECTIONS

Cut out 2 evenly sized square pieces of cardboard. Size the pieces to how large you want your puzzle to be.

On 1 piece of the cardboard, draw your design for the puzzle you want to make. To draw the turtle, start by drawing the shell first, and then draw the head and flippers.

On the shell, draw sections to create 7 puzzle pieces. The middle piece won't be a puzzle piece, but the 6 outer sections will.

Have an adult cut out the pieces of your puzzle with a craft knife. The shapes that are cut out will become your puzzle pieces! Leave the middle piece of the shell intact.

Glue the cut-out cardboard piece to the second square cardboard piece to create your puzzle.

Decorate and paint your puzzle pieces! You can make the turtle head and flippers green and the shell pieces different colors.

To add bubble wrap to the puzzle pieces, cut out a bubble wrap piece that is the same size as your shell piece. Paint the bubble wrap and once dry, glue it on top of your puzzle piece.

Now your puzzle is ready to play with!

 TRY THIS! Build a rainbow, fish or sun cardboard puzzle.

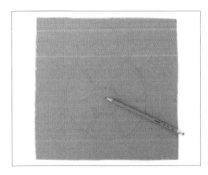

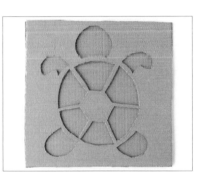

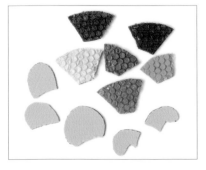

Rainbow and Cloud with Pop Tabs

Turn pop tabs into art! This colorful rainbow cloud will surely put a smile on your face! Hang this colorful cloud and rainbow in front of your window or on the wall.

MATERIALS

Milk carton piece or cardboard

Pencil

Scissors

Hole puncher

9 pop tabs

Blue acrylic paint

Paintbrush

Fishing line

Cotton balls

Glue

Googly eyes

Red, orange, yellow, green, blue and purple cardstock

Twine or string

DIRECTIONS

Draw the shape of a cloud on the milk carton piece or cardboard. Cut out the cloud.

Punch 3 holes where the raindrops will go. Add a hole to the top of the cloud for hanging.

Paint the pop tabs blue and let them dry.

Cut a small piece of fishing line (approximately 9 inches [23 cm] long). Loop it through 1 of the bottom holes of the cloud and tie it. Tie the fishing line around 1 pop tab. Continue to tie the pop tabs together with fishing line until you have 3 pop tabs hanging down.

Repeat for each hole punch so you have 9 raindrops.

Glue cotton balls onto the cloud and glue googly eyes on top of the cotton.

Create your rainbow by drawing and cutting out a rainbow shape from each color of cardstock. Make red the largest and then use it to trace the next color. When cutting the next color, make it slightly smaller (approximately 0.5 inch [1.25 cm]) than the previous color. Then glue all of the colors together. Trim the middle and glue to the back of the cloud.

Thread a piece of twine through the hole at the top of the cloud. Make sure it is behind the rainbow, and then tie it. Hang your creation on the wall or in front of a window!

 TRY THIS! Try making other pop tab art like flowers or butterflies.

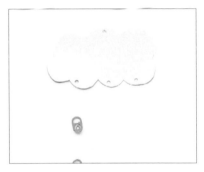

Build Your Own Marble Maze

Can you make the marble move from start to finish? How quickly can you complete the maze? Challenge your friends to see who can finish the maze the fastest!

MATERIALS

Paper rolls

Ice pop sticks

White and colored acrylic paint

Paintbrush

Scissors

Cardboard box

Pouch bottle caps

Hot glue gun and hot-melt glue sticks

Black marker

Marble

✔ RECYCLING TIP!

Use reusable bags when shopping.

DIRECTIONS

Paint the paper rolls and sticks to give the maze some color. Let the pieces dry. Cut some paper rolls to a smaller size (approximately 2 inches [5 cm] long) if desired. Trim down a paper towel roll for the starting point.

Paint the inside of the cardboard box white. If you do not have a box, you can use a cereal box and cut out 1 side of the box.

Lay out the design of your maze with the paper rolls, sticks and pouch bottle caps. You can use paper rolls as the starting point. Then finish the marble maze inside a stick area.

Once your design is laid out, have an adult help to hot glue everything down. Create the maze's starting position by writing START with the black marker. Add a FINISH spot for where the maze ends.

See how quickly you can get the marble from start to finish!

TRY THIS! Try making another design that is more difficult! Add more sticks or obstacles to the maze.

 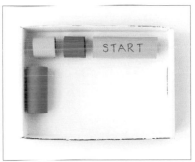 

Silly Tissue Box Monster

This silly, googly-eyed monster will put a smile on your face. This is a fun and simple Halloween craft. You can make this monster to play with or to store your favorite items inside.

MATERIALS

Tissue box

White and other color acrylic paint

Paintbrush

Black marker

Googly eyes

Glue

Scissors

Ice pop sticks (optional)

Craft knife (optional)

White paper or cardstock

Large pom-poms

DIRECTIONS

Pull out any plastic inner lining inside the tissue box before you start.

Paint the outside of the tissue box with white to prime the box. Adding white will make sure the design of the tissue box doesn't show through the paint.

Once dry, paint the outside of the tissue box a color of your choice, and paint the inside a different color.

Outline around the "mouth" of the monster (the opening of the tissue box) with a black marker. This will make the mouth pop more.

Glue large googly eyes to the top of the tissue box. You can add 1, 2, 3 or more eyes!

For the purple box pictured here, cut 1 stick in half. Paint the pieces purple and let them dry. Glue 2 small googly eyes to the sticks. Have an adult make 2 small slit marks at the top of the box with the craft knife to push the sticks in.

Cut out large teeth from paper or white cardstock. Glue the teeth to the inside of the tissue box mouth.

Give your monsters a little more character by gluing some large pom-poms to the top of the tissue boxes.

TRY THIS! Make eyes out of pom-poms or egg cartons instead.

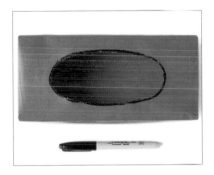

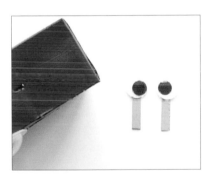

Rainbow Jellyfish

Create this colorful rainbow jellyfish from cardboard and some leftover bubble wrap. Hang it up to add a little ocean fun to a room. You can even use tissue paper, streamers or ribbon for the tentacles!

MATERIALS

Cardboard

Small paper plate or jar

Pencil

Scissors

Red, orange, yellow, green, blue and purple acrylic paint

Paintbrush

Bubble wrap

Googly eyes

Glue

Black marker

String (optional)

✔ RECYCLING TIP!

Encourage friends and family to properly recycle. Every little bit can add up to be a big difference!

DIRECTIONS

Trace a half circle on the cardboard. You can use a small paper plate or a jar to trace the shape. Cut out the half circle.

Paint the half circle the color of your choice. Let it dry.

Cut out 6 strips of bubble wrap that are the same size and length. Paint these in the colors of the rainbow. Let them dry.

Glue googly eyes onto your cardboard piece and draw a mouth with a black marker.

Glue the bubble wrap strips to the back of the cardboard in the order of the rainbow: red, orange, yellow, green, blue and purple.

Glue some string to the back of the jellyfish if you want to hang it up.

TRY THIS! Make a rainbow from bubble wrap and cardboard.

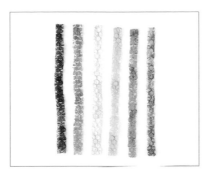

Shoebox Aquarium

Bring your own undersea world to life with stones, seashells, bubble wrap and pipe cleaners! Give some brightly colored fish a new home in this shoebox aquarium. And you can use the fish template in this book to easily make the fish!

MATERIALS

Shoebox

Turquoise acrylic paint or cardstock

White acrylic paint (optional)

Paintbrush

Bubble wrap

Scissors

Extra-strong glue

Green pipe cleaners

Stones

Hot glue gun and hot-melt glue sticks

Shells

Fish template (page 153)

Pencil

Red, yellow and orange cardstock

Fishing line or string

Tape

Googly eyes

Black marker (optional)

DIRECTIONS

Paint the inside of your shoebox with the turquoise acrylic paint (or you can cover the inside with turquoise cardstock). If the inside of your shoebox is a dark color, you may need to paint with white paint first before painting the blue on top.

Cut out a piece of bubble wrap that will fit in the backdrop of the aquarium. Lightly paint this with the turquoise paint. Let it dry and then glue it to the inside of the shoebox.

Cut a bunch of different-sized green pipe cleaners. Make 2 bunches and glue these to the sides of the aquarium scene. Have an adult help to hot glue some stones in front of the pipe cleaners. Then glue some shells in front of the pipe cleaners and tuck them behind the stones.

To make the fish, trace the fish template on page 153 on the colored cardstock. Cut out 2 fish for every fish you want to hang and 1 fish for every one you wish to glue to the backdrop.

For the fish you want to hang, tape a piece of fishing line to 1 side of the fish. Then glue another fish on top of this fish, sandwiching the fishing line between the 2 fish.

Glue a googly eye to each fish. You can also add scales or smiley faces to the fish with a marker!

Tape the fishing line to the top of the shoebox. Glue other fish to the back of the aquarium.

TRY THIS! Add some more sea creatures by creating a crab from a seashell or adding a paper seahorse.

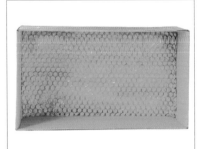
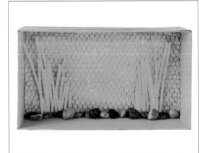

Shoebox Winter Diorama

Turn a shoebox into a winter arctic scene! Use the templates provided to add trees, a polar bear and an arctic fox to your diorama. Use your creativity to decorate the shoebox with cotton balls, cardboard and paper.

MATERIALS

Tree, polar bear and fox templates (page 149)

Pencil

Cardboard

Scissors

Green, dark blue and white acrylic paint

Paintbrush

Extra-strong glue

White cardstock

Shoebox

Dark blue cardstock (optional)

Cotton balls

Cotton swab

DIRECTIONS

To make the trees, trace the tree template on page 149 on the cardboard.

Cut out the cardboard trees and paint them green. Let them dry.

In order to make your trees stand up, you'll need an extra piece of cardboard you can glue down to the shoebox. Cut out a small rectangular piece of cardboard and fold it in half. Then glue this small piece of cardboard to the back side of the trees.

Trace the polar bear and arctic fox templates on page 149 on the white cardstock. If you want to make the polar bear stand up, add 2 small rectangle cardstock strips to the back of its feet. To do this, cut out a small rectangular strip from the white cardstock and then fold this in half. Then glue to the back of the polar bear template.

Add your arctic elements to the shoebox! Paint the inside of the empty shoebox dark blue. Or you can cover the inside with dark blue cardstock. Glue cotton balls around the outside and inside of the shoebox to decorate it.

To make snowflakes on the backdrop of your shoebox, take a cotton swab and dip it in white paint, and then dot it on the backdrop. Finally, glue your trees, polar bear and fox down.

 TRY THIS! Make a fall or summer diorama. What animals would you add into the box?

ADULT ASSISTANCE REQUIRED

Cereal Box Farm Puppet Theater

Create your own farm puppet theater with some paper, cardboard and your own imagination! You can even add toy tractors to your scene to bring your farm puppet theater to life! What farm songs will you sing while your animals are on stage?

MATERIALS

For the Farm

Large cereal box

Scissors or craft knife

White and red acrylic paint

Paintbrush

Cardboard

Pencil

10 regular ice pop sticks

14 small craft sticks

Extra-strong glue

For the Puppets

Small paint bottle

White, pink (2 shades), yellow, red and orange cardstock

Pencil

Scissors

3 ice pop sticks

White paint

Paintbrush

Black marker

Extra-strong glue

Small googly eyes

DIRECTIONS

To make the puppet theater, cut the back out of the large cereal box. Have an adult help with the cutting if using a craft knife.

Cut a square out of the front, leaving about 3 inches (7.6 cm) on each side for the barn doors.

Paint the cereal box white. This will prevent the design of the cereal box from shining through the paint.

Once dry, paint the whole cereal box red. You may need a few coats. Let it dry.

To make the barn top, measure the size of the cereal box on the cardboard. Then draw the barn top and cut it out.

Paint the top barn piece red. Let it dry.

Paint 10 regular sticks and 14 small sticks white. Let them dry.

Glue 4 regular and 2 small sticks to each side of the barn. Make a rectangle with the sticks and then make an "X" inside with the regular sticks.

To decorate the top of the barn, use 4 small sticks and 2 regular sticks. Glue these around the outside top edge. Then glue a rectangle and "X" in the center with 6 small sticks. You may need to cut and trim some of the sticks to make them fit the cardboard.

Glue the top piece to the cereal box and you've got your barn puppet theater!

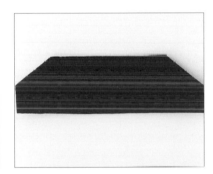

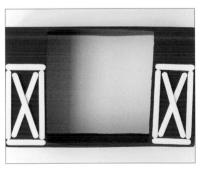

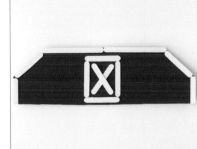

(continued)

Cereal Box Farm Puppet Theater (continued)

To make the puppets, trace around the bottom of a small paint bottle (or other round object) on the colored cardstock. Use the darker pink cardstock for the pig, white for the cow and yellow for the chicken. Cut out the circles. Paint the 3 regular sticks white or leave them plain.

To make the pig, cut a smaller circle from the lighter pink cardstock for the snout. Draw 2 small nostrils with the black marker. Cut out 2 ears from the lighter pink cardstock and glue them to the back of the head. Glue on 2 small googly eyes.

To make the cow, add a small pink circle for the mouth. Draw 2 small nostrils and a smile with the black marker. Glue on 2 small googly eyes.

Then draw some cow spots with the black marker. Finally, to make the ears, cut out a small ear shape from the white cardstock and glue a smaller pink piece on top. Glue the ears on.

To make the chicken, make a beak by folding a small piece of orange cardstock over. Draw a triangle and cut it out so that the beak will open up, and glue to the middle of the face. Glue on 2 small googly eyes. Cut out a red comb and glue it to the back of the chicken.

Glue your puppet heads to sticks.

TRY THIS! What other farm animal puppets can you make? How about a goat, sheep or horse?

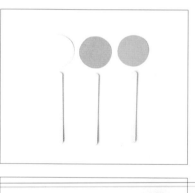

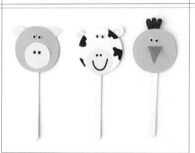

Awesome Cardboard Castle

Cardboard can become anything, but a castle is a classic craft that you have to try to make! With just one box and some paper rolls you can bring your own castle to life. Then bring your knights, princess and dragons to join their new home in the castle you made!

MATERIALS

1 large cardboard box at least 12" x 9" (30.5 x 23 cm)

Measuring tape

Scissors

Paint

Paintbrush

4 paper towel or wrapping paper rolls

Hot glue gun and hot-melt glue sticks

Brown and red cardstock

Extra-strong glue or tape

Small margarine container for tracing (optional)

4 toothpicks

(continued)

Awesome Cardboard Castle (continued)

Measure out the size you want your castle to be. Cut out 2 equally sized pieces from the cardboard box for the front and back walls. The front wall of the castle pictured is 12 inches (30.5 cm) wide by 9 inches (23 cm) tall.

Cut out 2 smaller pieces for the sides of the castle. The side wall dimensions for the castle pictured are 5.5 inches (14 cm) wide by 9 inches (23 cm) tall.

Make sure the sides are the same height.

Once you have your pieces, cut out the top of the castle walls in a tooth-shaped pattern. Measure out the spacing so that there is an even number of raised sections.

Cut a small door out of your front wall piece. Leave a little bit of the door attached so it will open slightly.

Paint the cardboard wall pieces light blue or any color you'd like. You can even leave the castle plain.

Paint 4 paper towel rolls the same color as the castle.

Have an adult help to hot glue 1 paper towel roll to each side of the front wall piece. Then cut out 2 small windows from brown cardstock. Glue the windows to the top of the paper rolls. Repeat this for the back wall piece.

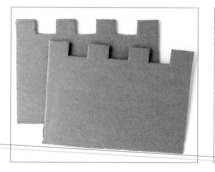

Stand the front wall piece up and have an adult help hot glue the side wall pieces to the paper rolls. Then hot glue the back wall piece to the side wall pieces.

For the finishing touch, make the peaks of the towers. Trace a large circular item (like a small margarine container) on the brown cardstock and cut out 4 circles. Make a slit in the circles and then roll them to form cones. Trim off any excess paper. Glue or tape the paper together to keep the cones in place. Then glue the cones to the top of the paper towel rolls.

To add the flags, cut out 4 small flags from red cardstock. Glue or tape these to a toothpick and then glue to the top of the cones.

TRY THIS! Make a smaller or larger castle by experimenting with different recycled materials and paper rolls.

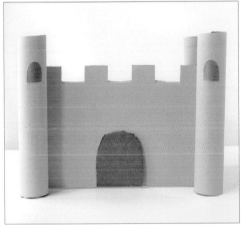

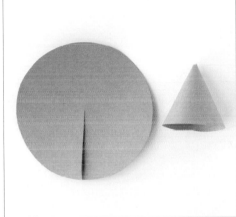

Simple Princess Crown

Play princess and dragons with your very own cardboard crown!
You can make different colors, shapes and sizes. Keep the crown simple
or add as many craft gems as you'd like.

MATERIALS

Cardboard

Pencil

Measuring tape

Scissors

Hole puncher

Acrylic paint

Paintbrush

Extra-strong glue

Craft gems

White polyester elastic

Hot glue gun and hot-melt
glue sticks

DIRECTIONS

Draw a design for your crown on the cardboard. You can look up pictures of crowns to get inspiration for what shape and size you want your crown to be.

Measure the front of your head so you know how wide to make the crown. Make it a little larger than the size of your head.

Once you're happy with the size of the crown, cut it out. Then make a hole punch on the bottom sides of the crown.

Paint the crown and let it dry. You may need to paint a few coats.

Glue craft gems or other decorations to your crown.

To add the elastic, first measure the size of your head. Cut a piece of elastic that will fit around your head and leave a little extra on the ends to glue down.

Loop the elastic through the holes and have an adult help to hot glue it down to the other side of the elastic. Then do the same to the other side.

Now your crown is ready to test for size! If the crown is not tight enough, trim your elastic band to make it smaller.

TRY THIS! Make matching princess and prince crowns.

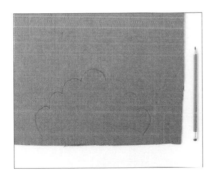

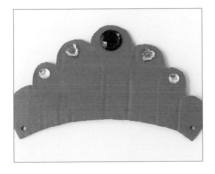

Cool Superhero Mask

POW! ZAP! BAM! Become the superhero of your dreams with these easy-to-make cardboard superhero masks! Use the template on page 151 to design your own mask. You can even make these with paper or felt!

MATERIALS

Thin cardboard from a cereal box or granola snack box

Pencil

Superhero mask template (page 151)

Scissors

Acrylic paint

Paintbrush

Hole puncher

Foam star stickers

Yellow cardstock (optional)

Glue (optional)

Measuring tape

White polyester elastic

Hot glue gun and hot-melt glue sticks

DIRECTIONS

Trace the template on page 151 on the thin cardboard. Trace on the side of the cardboard with the graphic so this will be hidden when wearing the mask.

Cut out the mask. For the eyeholes, you can bend the cardboard slightly to make a slit mark with scissors. Then cut the eyeholes out.

Paint the superhero mask in any color that you'd like. Red, blue and yellow are great superhero colors!

Punch a hole on both sides of the mask.

Decorate the mask with foam stars. You can also draw lightning bolts on yellow cardstock and glue them to the sides of the mask.

To add the elastic, first measure the size of your head. Cut a piece of elastic so that it will fit with a little extra on the ends to glue down.

Loop the elastic through the holes and have an adult help to hot glue it down to the other side of the elastic. Then do the same to the other side. If the mask is too big or too small, trim or lengthen the elastic to fit. Now you can wear your mask!

TRY THIS! Make matching superhero cuffs from paper rolls. Cut a slit in the paper roll and then decorate with matching colors and designs.

Cookie-Cutter Christmas Ornaments

HO, HO, HO! Christmas bells are ringing, and the Christmas tree is ready to be put up! Decorate your Christmas tree with these handmade cardboard Christmas ornaments. These couldn't be easier to make with cookie-cutters as your template!

MATERIALS

Cookie-cutters

Cardboard

Pencil

Scissors

Hole puncher

Red, white, green and brown paint

Paintbrush

Red felt

Extra-strong glue

Green yarn

Red and white pom-poms

Yellow foam star sticker

3 black buttons

Black foam or cardstock

Red and orange cardstock

Black marker

Twine

DIRECTIONS

Trace your favorite Christmas cookie-cutters on the cardboard. Cut out the different shapes.

Punch a hole at the top of the cardboard shapes.

Paint the snowman and candy cane white. Paint the stocking red and the Christmas tree green.

To make the candy cane, cut out strips of red felt and glue them diagonally to the cardboard.

To make the Christmas tree, wrap green yarn around the cardboard. Decorate with red pom-poms and a yellow foam star sticker. Paint the Christmas tree trunk brown.

To make the stocking, glue white pom-poms to the top of the stocking. You can also use cotton balls.

To make the snowman, glue on the 3 black buttons. Glue a piece of black foam or cardstock to the top to make the hat, and then trim around the edge to fit it to the snowman's head. Add a red cardstock strip for the brim of the hat. Add a nose by cutting one out from the orange cardstock. Draw the eyes and mouth with the black marker.

Add twine to the ornaments for hanging.

 TRY THIS! Use the cookie-cutters to make new Christmas cards from old Christmas cards. Cut out shapes from the old cards and glue to a new card.

CHAPTER SIX

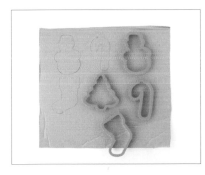

Easy Ice Pop Stick Projects

When you get that box of 30 ice pops or ice cream bars this summer, don't forget to save the sticks! They are great for making baskets, puzzles and frames. Paint them and turn them into cool new creations like fun airplanes, sailboats and more!

STORING TIPS: Wash the sticks with soap and water and lay them flat on a towel to dry. Store them in a reusable bag or recycled jar.

Simple Sailboat

Sail away with this ice pop stick sailboat. Make it for fun or even as a STEM challenge to see if you can get it to float! Make several of them and have a race to see whose sailboat wins.

MATERIALS

9 regular ice pop sticks

Red, yellow, blue and white acrylic paint

Paintbrush

Extra-strong glue

2 small craft sticks

Hot glue gun and hot-melt glue sticks

Cardstock

Scissors

DIRECTIONS

Paint 6 regular sticks red, yellow or blue to make the base of the boat. Let them dry.

Glue the sticks together side by side. Glue 2 extra sticks to the back to help them stay together.

Paint 1 regular stick and the 2 small sticks white. Let them dry.

Get an adult to help hot glue the regular stick standing up on top of the base of the boat with the 2 small ones on each side for support (see photo).

Cut out 2 triangle-shaped sails from the cardstock. Use the first triangle shape to trace and cut out the second one.

Glue the sails on each side of the white stick that is standing up on the boat.

 TRY THIS! Add some recycled foam or corks to the bottom of the boat to see if you can make it float on water!

Fun Airplane

Turn a few ice pop sticks and a clothespin into an airplane. Create your own airport scene with different colored airplanes and a runway. Add some string or fishing line around them and you can even hang them up.

MATERIALS

2 regular ice pop sticks

2 small craft sticks

Clothespin

Paint

Paintbrush

Small wooden circle, white pom-pom or white button

Extra-strong glue

Colored tape

DIRECTIONS

Paint the regular and small sticks any color you want. Paint the clothespin a different color.

Glue the small wooden circle to the middle of one of the small sticks to make the propeller center. You can paint this white or a different color. You can also use a white pom-pom or a small white button.

Add some colored tape to the ends of one regular stick and the other small stick. You can make the tape straight or diagonal. You can also paint these designs on.

Glue the regular sticks on the top and bottom of the clothespin about 0.5 inch (1.25 cm) from the front of the clothespin. Glue one of the small sticks to the back on top of the clothespin.

Glue the small stick with the propeller diagonally to the front of the clothespin.

TRY THIS! Make an airport runway out of cardboard. Cut a rectangular strip of cardboard, paint it black and add white strips of paper.

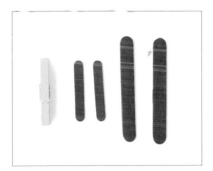

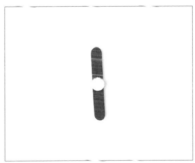

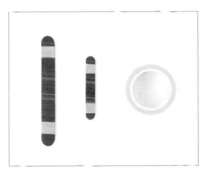

Easy Paper Fan

Cool off in the summer with this easy-to-make ice pop stick paper fan!
Make a bunch and bring them to hand out to friends and family
at your next outdoor event.

MATERIALS

2 ice pop sticks

White paint

Paintbrush

Extra-strong glue

Colored cardstock

Scissors

DIRECTIONS

Paint the sticks white. Let them dry. You can also leave them unpainted.

Glue the bottoms of the sticks together in a "V" shape. The shape you create will determine how large your fan will be. If you want a larger fan, make the "V" shape wider.

Cut out a long rectangular strip of cardstock.

Start at one end of the paper and fold over a strip about 0.5 inch (1.25 cm) in size. Then fold another 0.5 inch (1.25 cm) the opposite way. Keep going until the full strip looks like an accordion.

Glue each end of the paper to the stick ends. You may need to trim your paper if there is too much to fit inside the fan.

TRY THIS! Make a paper fan that opens and closes by using cardboard instead of ice pop sticks. Then add a paper fastener at the base so you can open and close the fan.

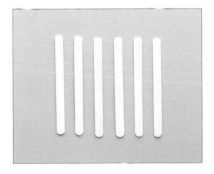
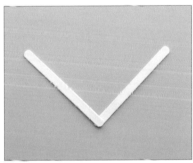

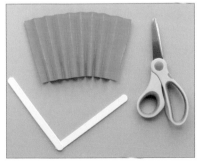
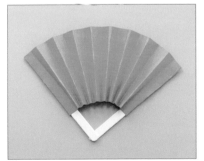

Weather Puzzle

Did you know you can make your own puzzle with ice pop sticks? Design your own puzzle and see if your friends and family can put it together. Store it in a travel bag for trips on the road!

MATERIALS

10 ice pop sticks
White and other colored paint
Paintbrush
Masking tape
Pencil
Black permanent marker

 **RECYCLING TIP!**

Use reusable lunch containers instead of plastic sandwich bags.

DIRECTIONS

Paint the sticks white. You can also leave them plain and skip this step.

Line up the sticks side by side and tape the back to keep them together.

Lightly sketch out your design with the pencil. Draw a sun, cloud, rainbow or anything else you can imagine!

Paint your design. Paint the sun yellow and the cloud blue. For the rainbow, carefully paint each block of color.

Once dry, use a black permanent marker to draw on the eyes and mouth, if needed.

Dip the end of a paintbrush handle in light pink paint and add some cheeks to the sides of any faces, if desired.

Once fully dry, you can remove the masking tape from the back.

Now test out your new puzzle! How quickly can you solve it?

TRY THIS! Make a puzzle using a personalized photo. Glue the photo on a row of sticks and then cut out the pieces.

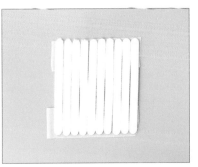
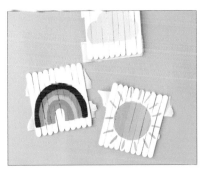

Boredom Buster Jar

Bust summer or weekend boredom blues with your own activity inspiration jar! Make the jar as a gift or simply for your whole family to enjoy. You can even color-code the activities to make choosing an activity even easier.

MATERIALS

30 or more ice pop sticks

Acrylic paint in different colors

Paintbrush

Black permanent marker

Jar

TRY THIS!

Make a chore jar and add family chores to sticks for family members to pick out each week.

DIRECTIONS

Paint the sticks different colors. Start with the colors of the rainbow and do 5 of each color: red, orange, yellow, green, blue and purple.

Decide if you want to group the activities by color. For example, you can do green for outdoor activities, orange for sports, yellow for indoor activities, purple for excursions and blue for crafts or creations. Write down the activities on the sticks with the marker.

There are endless ideas for activities you can add into your boredom jar. When you think of new ones, just create another stick and drop it in.

Choosing a stick is easy! Close your eyes and choose one at random or choose from your favorite color.

Here are some activity ideas you can add to the sticks:

- Fly a kite
- Blow bubbles
- Play with sidewalk chalk
- Collect wildflowers
- Read a book
- Play hopscotch
- Play hide-and-go-seek
- Play tag
- Make slime
- Play with playdough
- Write a story
- Play frisbee
- Do a science experiment

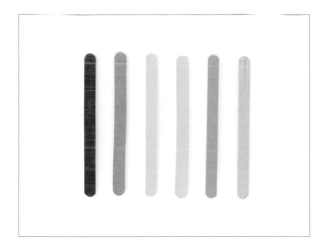

Personalized Trinket Box

Create a trinket or jewelry box from ice pop sticks. Add your extra craft supplies, coins, jewelry or other trinkets to the box for safekeeping. You can make the box any size you'd like. Customize the box with your own unique designs and favorite colors, too!

MATERIALS

48 ice pop sticks*

Acrylic paint

Paintbrush

Extra-strong glue

Embellishments such as paper flowers, buttons or gems

You'll need 48 sticks to make the small trinket box pictured here. If you want a larger box, you'll need 4 extra sticks for each layer you want to add.

DIRECTIONS

Paint the sticks and let them dry.

Create the base of the box by lining up 11 sticks side by side. Then glue 1 stick horizontally on the top of the sticks and 1 on the bottom to hold all of the sticks together.

Glue 2 sticks to the sides. Continue gluing sticks on the top, bottom and sides until you are happy with the height of the box.

Make the lid of the box the same way you made the base. Line up 11 sticks and glue an extra stick horizontally on the top and bottom of the lined-up sticks.

Decorate the lid. Glue 3 paper flowers and add buttons to the center of them. You can also decorate the lid to match your room or add your favorite designs and colors to it!

 **TRY THIS!** Decorate a small box or container with ice pop sticks. Glue the sticks vertically around the outside of the container.

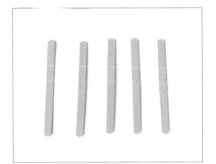

Magnet Frame

Make this easy frame from ice pop sticks! You can add a magnet to the back to stick to the fridge, or add string to hang it on a wall. Display your favorite picture, drawing or note.

MATERIALS

14 ice pop sticks

2 colors of acrylic paint

Paintbrush

Extra-strong glue

Small clothespin

Hot glue gun and hot-melt glue sticks

Buttons

Pom-poms or craft gems, for decorating (optional)

Magnet or string, for hanging

DIRECTIONS

Paint the sticks and let them dry.

Line up 10 sticks in a row. Alternate the colors as shown, like pink and orange or blue and green.

Glue 1 stick horizontally at the top and 1 at the bottom of the row of sticks. This will keep all of the sticks together.

Glue 1 stick vertically on top of the horizontal sticks on each side to finish the frame.

Paint a small clothespin and have an adult help you to hot glue it to the top of your frame.

Decorate the outside of the frame by gluing a button on each corner. You can also add pom-poms or craft gems.

Add a magnet to the back if you want to stick it on the fridge or glue string to the back for hanging.

TRY THIS! Glue an additional stick at a 45-degree angle to the back to make the frame stand up on its own.

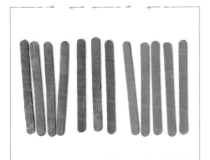

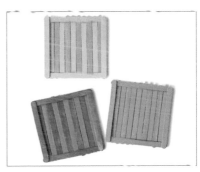

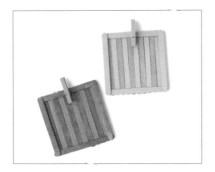

ADULT ASSISTANCE REQUIRED

Colorful Easter Basket

Save your favorite Easter eggs in your own handmade Easter basket! When Easter is done, you can use this simple basket to store your favorite items like craft supplies, small toys or photos.

MATERIALS

47 ice pop sticks

White, pink, orange and green acrylic paint

Paintbrush

Hot glue gun and hot-melt glue sticks

DIRECTIONS

Paint the sticks in the following way: 8 white, 16 pink, 12 orange and 11 green. Let them dry.

To make the base of the basket, place 11 sticks together side by side as shown. Have an adult help to hot glue the sticks together. Glue 2 pink sticks horizontally, 1 on the top and 1 on the bottom. Then glue 1 pink stick vertically on each side.

To make the basket sides, line up the colored sticks to fit the width of the base. Space out 6 colored sticks evenly and then have an adult help hot glue 2 white sticks on top (one closer to the top and one closer to the bottom). The white sticks will hold the whole piece together. Repeat this step to create 4 sides.

Have an adult help hot glue the side pieces to the base of the basket. Glue each side on one by one.

✂ **TRY THIS!** Add a handle to your basket with some pipe cleaners and twine wrapped around it.

CHAPTER SEVEN

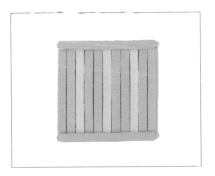

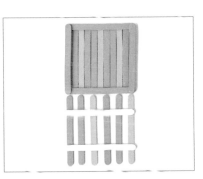
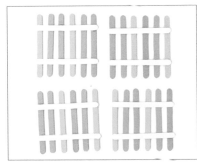

Awesome Jars, Bottles and More

Save pickle and Mason jars and turn them into something new, like a beautiful Spring Globe (page 120) or a cool Dinosaur Terrarium (page 124). Then reimagine other materials like milk cartons, margarine containers and bottle caps to create colorful bird feeders, birthday cakes and more!

STORING TIPS: Make sure to thoroughly wash out the jars. If you have trouble getting adhesive off of a jar, let it soak in some soapy water. Then scrub with a scoured sponge. Place smaller jars inside larger jars to save space, and keep a reusable bag in your kitchen to easily place pop tabs and bottle caps in.

Mason Jar Spring Globe

Create a small spring scene inside a Mason jar. This easy spring craft makes a great gift for Mother's Day. Or you can make these beautiful jars to decorate your room or home.

MATERIALS

Fabric or paper flowers or butterflies

Moss

Stones (optional)

Mason jar

Sticks

Scissors

Hot glue gun and hot-melt glue sticks

Decorative bird (optional)

DIRECTIONS

Gather the supplies you want to put in your spring globe, such as small rocks, moss, fabric flowers, fabric butterflies or other items you have around the home.

Trim or cut the sticks with scissors if needed so they will fit inside the jar. You can add 1 or 2 sticks depending on the size of the sticks and the jar.

Have an adult help hot glue the paper or fabric butterflies to the stick. (If you'd like to use paper flowers or butterflies, you can use the templates on page 151.)

Have an adult help hot glue the stick to the inside of the jar's lid. Glue fabric flowers around the stick and glue moss to the inside of the lid. You can add stones or other decorations to your jar if you'd like, too.

Place the lid on the jar and tightly twist it on. Stand the jar upside down so that the lid is on the bottom.

You can also add an extra decoration to the top of the jar as a finishing touch, such as a small decorative bird.

TRY THIS! Make a bird version with a small birdhouse inside and birds on the sticks.

Smell Jar Game

Can you guess the smell? This simple game is so easy to set up. Stump your family and friends with different smells and see who can guess the most!

MATERIALS

5 or more small jars or baby food jars

Acrylic paint in white and other colors

Paintbrush

Items to place in your smell jars (see lists on the next page)

Paper bag

Scissors

Rubber bands

Pencil

DIRECTIONS

Paint the jars with a white base coat. This will allow your colored paint to go on easier. Let them dry.

Paint your jars different colors. You can paint one for each color of the rainbow: red, orange, yellow, green, blue and purple. Let them dry.

Fill the jars with different items to smell. Use the items listed or other things you have around the house.

To cover the jars, cut small squares from the paper bag. Place each square on top of each jar and secure them with rubber bands.

With the pencil, punch a few holes in the jar coverings. You'll need quite a few holes to smell what's inside the jar. Don't worry about making too many holes; you won't be able to easily tell what's in the jar.

To play the game, label each jar with a number or by color. Have participants smell each jar and write down their guesses. Once they are done guessing, see how many they guessed right. The person who guessed the most smells correctly wins the game!

SMELLS TO TRY

Food Smells: Cinnamon, lemon, lime, chili powder, mint, parsley, chocolate, orange peels, peppermints, coffee beans, spices

Non-Food Smells: Pencil shavings, grass, lavender, pine needles, toothpaste, soap

TRY THIS! Make a summer-themed smell jar game! Put items in your jar that remind you of summer, like lemons for lemonade, grass, flowers and more!

Dinosaur Terrarium

Turn some old jars into a prehistoric wonderland. You can create your own dinosaur-land to display in your room or to give to your dinosaur-crazed friend. And if you're new to gardening, this is a great way to learn how to take care of a plant!

MATERIALS

Large jar

Small pebbles

Succulent plant

Soil

Moss

Small dinosaur toys

Pipette (optional)

✔ RECYCLING TIP!

Rinse out any containers before recycling. Items like peanut butter and jam jars need to be rinsed thoroughly or they can contaminate other items.

DIRECTIONS

A large pickle jar is great for this project. Choosing a jar with a wide mouth will make it easier to plant and fit in a small dinosaur.

Fill the bottom of the jar with small pebbles. This will provide some drainage for the water since the jar does not have holes in the bottom of it.

Add the succulent on top. Add extra soil around the plant to fill the jar.

Add a little bit of moss on top of the soil around the succulent.

Add the toy dinosaur. With a much larger jar you can fit more than one dinosaur, some larger stones and a few different kinds of succulents!

To care for your succulent, reference the care instructions included with the plant when purchased. Most succulents need to be watered at least once per week. Pour enough water to get the soil wet, but not too much so that it pools at the bottom of the jar. You can use a pipette to water the plant, and it's a great way to know how much water to give each time.

TRY THIS! Make a large dinosaur terrarium from an old fish bowl.

Tissue Paper Jar Luminaire

Upcycle an old food or Mason jar into a beautiful stained-glass luminaire. You can simply paint the jar or you can glue on tissue paper to create a stained-glass effect. Then add a flameless candle inside the jar to turn it into a luminaire.

MATERIALS

Tissue paper

Scissors

Paintbrush

Decoupage glue such as Mod Podge®

Jar

Flameless candle (optional)

DIRECTIONS

Cut the tissue paper into small squares that are the same size. You can also buy precut small square tissue paper at most craft and dollar stores.

With the paintbrush, apply a thin layer of decoupage glue to the jar. Layer the tissue paper over the jar. To make the rainbow jar, start with a row of red at the top and work your way down with the different colors of the rainbow.

Keep layering the tissue paper until the jar is covered.

With a clean brush, gently add a thin layer of decoupage glue on top of the whole jar. This will provide an extra protective layer.

Add the flameless candle inside the jar and enjoy. Or add in some trinkets if you want to use the jar for storage!

Safety note: Ensure your flameless candle has screws to secure the battery and keep out of reach of small children due to the button batteries included inside.

 TRY THIS! Try lightly painting the jar with diluted paint instead.

Silly Face Jars

Create some funny and silly face jars to hold wildflowers, pencils or even a small succulent plant. Create one or a whole set of matching silly face jars!

MATERIALS

Small jar or baby food jars

White and other colored acrylic paint

Paintbrush

Googly eyes

Extra-strong glue

Black permanent marker

Items to put inside your jar, such as flowers, stationary supplies, a succulent and rocks (optional)

✔️ **RECYCLING TIP!**

Use a reusable water bottle.

DIRECTIONS

Paint the jars with a white base coat. This will allow your colored paint to go on easier. Let them dry.

Paint the jars the colors of your choice. You will need a few coats to make the color even.

Once the paint is dry, decorate the jars. Glue on the googly eyes. Draw mouths with the black permanent marker. Make a large smiley face, a smirk face and a funny face with teeth sticking out.

Pick some dandelions or other wildflowers to place in the jars. You can also use the jars to store stationary supplies or even to plant a small succulent. If you want to plant a succulent in the jar, add some small rocks to the bottom of the jar first for drainage.

TRY THIS! Plant grass seed in your silly face jars and watch their "hair" grow.

Bottle Maracas

Did you know you can turn old plastic bottles into maracas? Making your own maracas is easier than you'd think! Experiment with different materials inside your bottles to see what types of sounds you can make.

MATERIALS

2 small plastic bottles*

White, red, green and yellow acrylic paint

Paintbrush

Masking tape

Dry beans

The bottles shown here are pomegranate juice bottles, which are fun because they have a unique shape.

DIRECTIONS

Paint the bottles with a white base coat. This will allow your colored paint to go on easier. Let them dry.

Wrap tape around the middle section of the bottles. This will help you paint the colors on straight.

Paint the top of the bottles green and the bottom red. You may need to paint a few coats. Let them dry.

Carefully peel off the tape and paint the middle yellow. Let them dry.

Fill the bottles with dry beans. You can experiment with adding more or fewer beans to see how the sound changes.

Finally, put the caps back on the bottles and twist them closed tightly.

TRY THIS! Put different materials inside the bottles to test the different sounds they will make. Try rice, different beans or small beads.

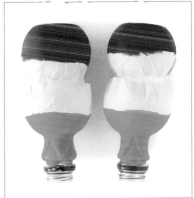

Spring Discovery Bottle

Create your own spring discovery bottle with some rice, sticks, paper flowers and toy bugs. Once the items are mixed up in the bottle, you can play a game trying to find them. Do you see a purple flower? How many flowers are in the bottle?

MATERIALS

Green acrylic paint

Small bowl

Rice

Wax paper

Plastic bottle

Funnel (optional)

Items to put inside your bottle, such as paper flowers, sticks, stones and toy insects

TRY THIS!

Make summer, fall and winter discovery bottles! What items would you place in each one?

DIRECTIONS

To make the rice "grass," add a small amount of green acrylic paint to the bowl and mix the rice around until it is covered in paint. Don't use too much paint or it will get clumpy. It's better to add a small amount to start with and then add more if needed.

Lay the rice out to dry on the wax paper.

Fill the plastic bottle halfway with rice. You can use a funnel to pour the rice inside the bottle, if needed.

Add in the items you want in your discovery bottle. You can use different colored paper flowers, sticks, stones (some large and small), small toy insects and more.

Fill the rest of the bottle with the remaining rice.

Twist the cap back on tightly. Shake the bottle around to mix everything together.

Now you can play a game with your friends to see which items they can spot in your bottle!

Milk Carton Bird Feeder

Attract some birds to your backyard with your very own recycled milk carton bird feeder. You can paint and decorate your bird feeder however you'd like! You can even use sticks for the roof or bark to make it blend into the tree.

MATERIALS

Milk or juice carton

White and other colored outdoor paint

Paintbrush

12 ice pop sticks

Pencil

Craft knife

Hot glue gun and weather-resistant hot-melt glue sticks

8 medium-size buttons

Dowel

Twine

Birdseed

DIRECTIONS

Push in the plastic milk carton opening inside the carton. (This is so that you can glue the sticks on top later.)

Paint the carton with a white base coat. This will allow your colored paint to go on easier. Let it dry.

Paint the carton any color you want. Let it dry.

While the carton is drying, paint the sticks to add to the top of the bird feeder.

Once the carton is dry, draw the window opening for the bird feeder with the pencil.

Have an adult cut out a window on each side of the feeder with the craft knife. Also have them cut a small hole for hanging and 2 holes on the bottom to place the wooden dowel through. The dowel is a little spot for the birds to rest on while they eat the birdseed!

Have an adult help to hot glue the sticks to the top to make the roof and hot glue the buttons to the top of the feeder. Add the dowel.

Thread the twine through the hole in the top of the feeder and tie it so you can hang it.

Add some birdseed and hang your bird feeder outside for the birds to enjoy!

 TRY THIS! Make a nature-inspired bird feeder by decorating the outside with sticks, stones and bark instead.

Bottle Cap Bees

Bzzzzzz . . . these buzzing bees are so easy to make!
Save some yellow bottle caps and then pretend to fly them
around their bubble wrap honeycomb.

MATERIALS

Pencil

Cardboard

Scissors

Extra-strong glue

Bubble wrap

Yellow paint

Paintbrush

Brown cardstock (optional)

Yellow bottle caps

Black permanent marker or
black paint

White cardstock

Small googly eyes

DIRECTIONS

With the pencil, draw a honeycomb shape on the cardboard and then cut it out.

Glue a piece of bubble wrap on top of the cardboard and cut around the edges to trim the bubble wrap to size.

Paint the bubble wrap yellow. Cut out a small circle from the brown cardstock or use cardboard. Glue this to the honeycomb to make the bees' entrance.

To make the bees, draw black stripes on the yellow bottle caps with the permanent marker. You can also paint on the stripes with black paint.

Cut out 2 small wings from the white cardstock for each bee and glue them to the top of the bottle caps. Glue on 2 small googly eyes for each bee.

You can glue your bees to the honeycomb or leave them loose to play with!

 TRY THIS! Try making other bottle cap insects like ladybugs or caterpillars.

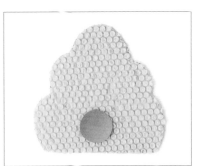

Pouch Bottle Cap Flower

Bottle caps can be turned into flowers with just a simple design! You can use pouch bottle caps, or you can also use regular bottle caps. Make some flowers for Mother's Day and give them to Grandma or Mom.

MATERIALS

Small jar or other round object (for tracing a circle)

Cardboard

Pencil

Scissors

Yellow paint

Paintbrush

7 pouch bottle caps or regular bottle caps, plus more for decoration

Hot glue gun and hot-melt glue sticks

Wooden dowel

Green paint

Green cardstock or construction paper

Extra-strong glue

Mason jar

TRY THIS!

What else can you create with pouch bottle caps? Can you make a flower scene on paper or add them to a card?

DIRECTIONS

Trace a circle on the cardboard using a small jar or other object. The circle shouldn't be larger than the flower you're making. Cut out the circle.

Paint the cardboard circle yellow. Let it dry.

Create your flower design using 6 pouch bottle caps or regular bottle caps for the petals. Add an extra one for the center. You can use pink, purple and red for the petals and yellow for the center.

Have an adult help to hot glue the pouch bottle caps to the cardboard. Start with the center and then add the petals.

Paint the wooden dowel green for the stem of your flower.

Have an adult help hot glue the wooden dowel to the back of the flower. If you want the flower to show on both sides, you'll need to glue another set of pouch bottle caps to the back of the flower.

Cut out a leaf for your flower from the green cardstock. Leave a little strip at the end of the leaf to wrap around your wooden dowel. Glue the leaf to the wooden dowel.

Place the flower in the Mason jar for display. Add extra pouch bottle caps into the jar for decoration.

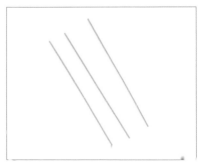

Rainbow Bottle Cap Paint Palette

Save all of those colorful bottle caps! Not only can you make art with them, but they also can be turned into a paint palette. You can make your own paint palette with cardboard and then use it to make some of the crafts in this book!

MATERIALS

Red, orange, yellow, green, blue and purple bottle caps

Cardboard or milk carton

Scissors

Hot glue gun and hot-melt glue sticks

Sponge (for cleaning up)

DIRECTIONS

If you want to include all of the colors of the rainbow on your paint palette, you'll need a red, orange, yellow, green, blue and purple bottle cap. Save any colorful bottle caps or ask friends and neighbors to save them for you. You can also use white, clear or any color bottle caps to make your paint palette.

Cut out a rectangular piece of cardboard for your base. Use the side of a milk carton instead of cardboard if you want your base to be water resistant, which makes clean-up easier!

Have an adult help to hot glue the bottle caps to your cardboard in the order of the rainbow. Glue the top of the caps down so that you can fill the inside of the caps with paint.

To clean the paint palette when done, use up as much of the paint on your project. Then take a slightly wet sponge and wipe off any excess paint inside the bottle caps. If you used a milk carton for the base, you can use the sponge on the base as well.

TRY THIS! Make a paint palette in the shape of a traditional paint palette and place the bottle caps in an upside-down "U" shape on the cardboard.

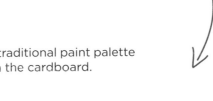

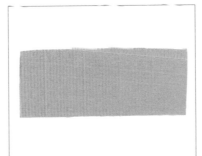

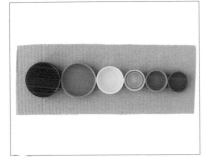

Margarine Container Birthday Cake

Save margarine containers and turn them into a beautiful pretend-play cake! Host your own birthday party with friends. Don't forget to sing "Happy Birthday!"

MATERIALS

2 margarine containers (1 needs to be smaller than the other)

White acrylic paint, or color of choice

Paintbrush

Pink and yellow tissue paper

Scissors

Extra-strong glue

Hot glue gun and hot-melt glue sticks

Pom-poms

Blue cardstock

Tape (optional)

DIRECTIONS

Paint the margarine containers white or another color for your cake. Because of the labels on the containers, you'll need to paint at least 2 coats to evenly cover the labels. Let them dry.

Cut a strip of pink tissue paper to decorate the margarine containers. The tissue paper shown already had a scalloped design to it. If you do not have this, you can cut out scallops from the tissue paper to make a similar design.

Glue the tissue paper to the top of each container with the opening of the container facing down as shown on the cake.

Have an adult help to hot glue the smaller container on top of the larger one.

Glue pom-poms around the top of each container on the cake. Use large pom-poms for the top and smaller ones on the bottom container.

To add the finishing touch, make paper candles to glue to the top of your cake. Cut out 3 small rectangle shapes (approximately 3 x 2 inches [7.5 x 5 cm] wide) from the blue cardstock. Roll the paper to form the shape of the candle. Glue or tape together. To make the candle flames, cut out some yellow tissue paper into a flame shape and then glue them into the paper candles.

Glue the candles to the top of the cake.

Now it's time to sing "Happy Birthday!"

 TRY THIS! Make a rectangular birthday cake from a small cardboard box or cereal box!

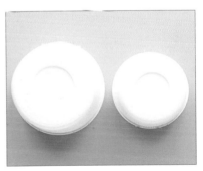

Plastic Container Suncatcher

Make your windows shine with color by creating your own suncatchers. Plastic containers are perfect for recycling into suncatchers because of their transparency, which lets the sun shine through!

MATERIALS

Plastic container

A round cookie cutter or container lid

Colored permanent markers

Scissors

Tissue paper

Glue

Paintbrush

Hole puncher (optional)

String or double-sided tape (optional)

TRY THIS!

What other suncatcher shapes can you make with recycled plastic containers? Try creating other shapes like stars or hearts!

DIRECTIONS

Use a plastic container with an area large enough to make your suncatcher. You can use the top of a plastic egg carton or the top of a plastic fruit container.

Trace the round cookie-cutter or container lid onto the plastic container with a colored permanent marker. Cut the circle out.

Add more permanent marker color around the edge of the circle shape to make a border.

Cut some pieces of tissue paper into small squares.

Glue the tissue paper to the back of the plastic circle. Layer the tissue paper pieces to make a stained-glass effect. Use a paintbrush to apply the glue.

Punch a hole at the top of the circle so you can thread string through if you want to hang the suncatcher in front of the window. Or you can use double-sided tape and tape it directly to the window.

ACKNOWLEDGMENTS

To my husband, who has always been my #1 supporter and fan.

To my kids, who inspire me every day to create and imagine new things.

To my parents and parents-in-law, for all of your support.

To Mom, Jenn, Tricia, Jaclyn, Laura and Melissa, for being my craft and photo critiques.

To all of my adorable kid models in this book—thanks for bringing the crafts to life.

To Ruxandra Serbanoiu—thank you for creating the designs that go with the crafts.

To my community of followers who follow and create the crafts we share.

To Marissa Giambelluca, Meg Baskis, Kylie Alexander and the entire Page Street team—thank you for making this book possible.

ABOUT THE AUTHOR

Kimberly McLeod is the creator of the popular kid's craft and activity website, The Best Ideas for Kids® (thebestideasforkids .com). The Best Ideas for Kids® has a community of over 2 million followers.

Kimberly lives just outside of Toronto, Ontario, Canada with her two kids and husband. She has a passion for creating and sharing kids craft projects. She loves to create projects that are easy, and she incorporates recycled materials as much as she can. She is also known for her handprint cards and crafts. Her work has been featured in *Woman's World* magazine and online media, including *Country Living* and *Good Housekeeping*.

To see more fun and easy craft ideas, visit thebestideasforkids.com or you can follow on Facebook at facebook.com/thebestideasforkids or on Instagram at @bestideasforkids.

SHARE YOUR CRAFTS WITH US!

We'd love to see all of the creations you make from this book! Share in our Facebook group (join at facebook.com/groups/ bestideasforkids) or tag us on Instagram with @bestideasforkids and use the hashtag #funandeasycrafting.

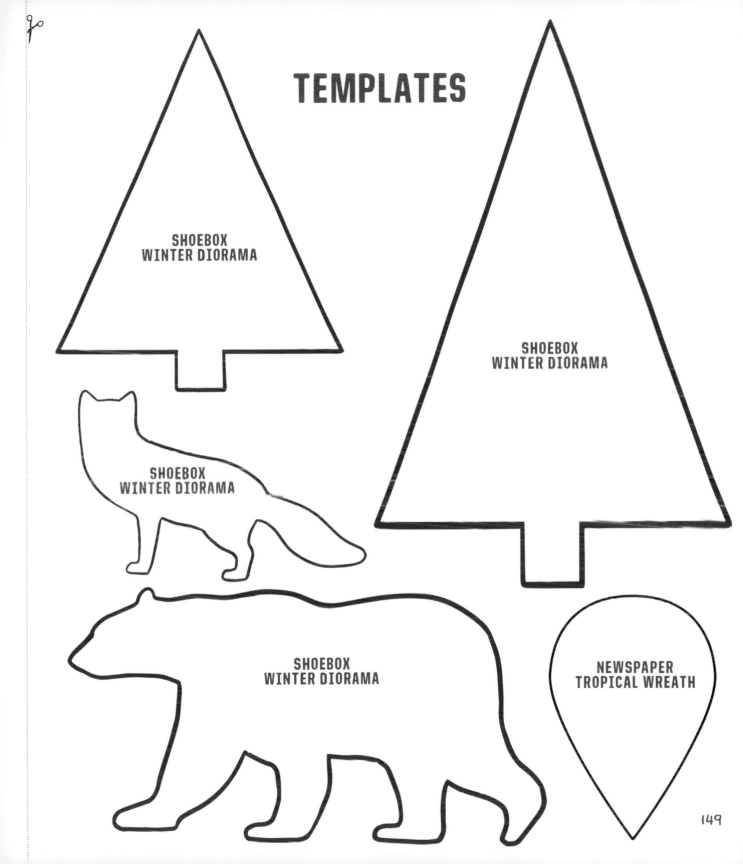

TEMPLATES

SHOEBOX
WINTER DIORAMA

SHOEBOX
WINTER DIORAMA

SHOEBOX
WINTER DIORAMA

SHOEBOX
WINTER DIORAMA

NEWSPAPER
TROPICAL WREATH

149

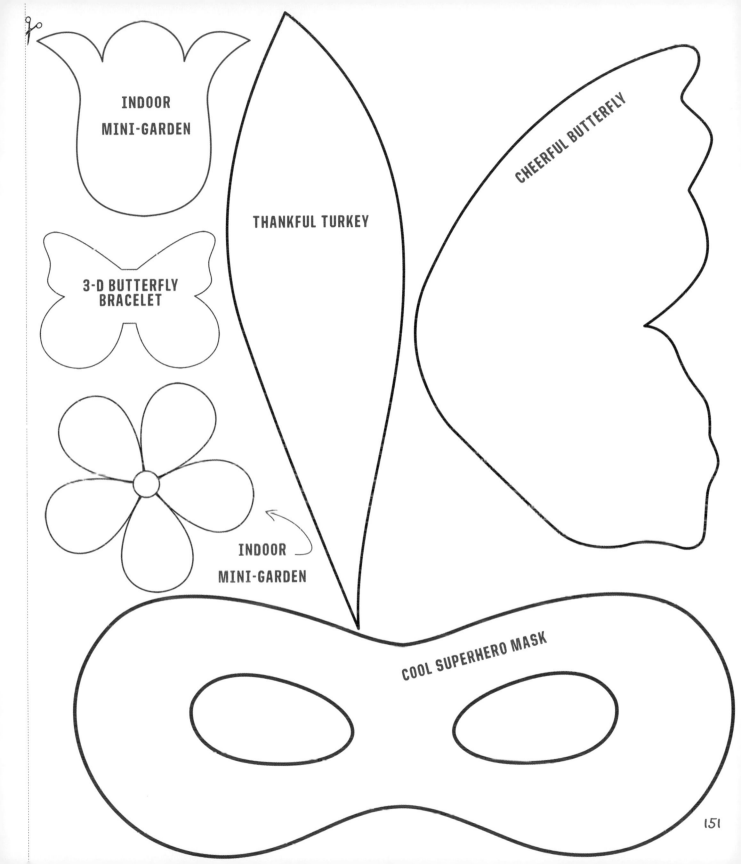

INDOOR
MINI-GARDEN

3-D BUTTERFLY
BRACELET

THANKFUL TURKEY

CHEERFUL BUTTERFLY

INDOOR
MINI-GARDEN

COOL SUPERHERO MASK

151

EASY
MONKEY
FACE

EASY MONKEY FACE

EASY MONKEY FACE

SHOEBOX
AQUARIUM

153

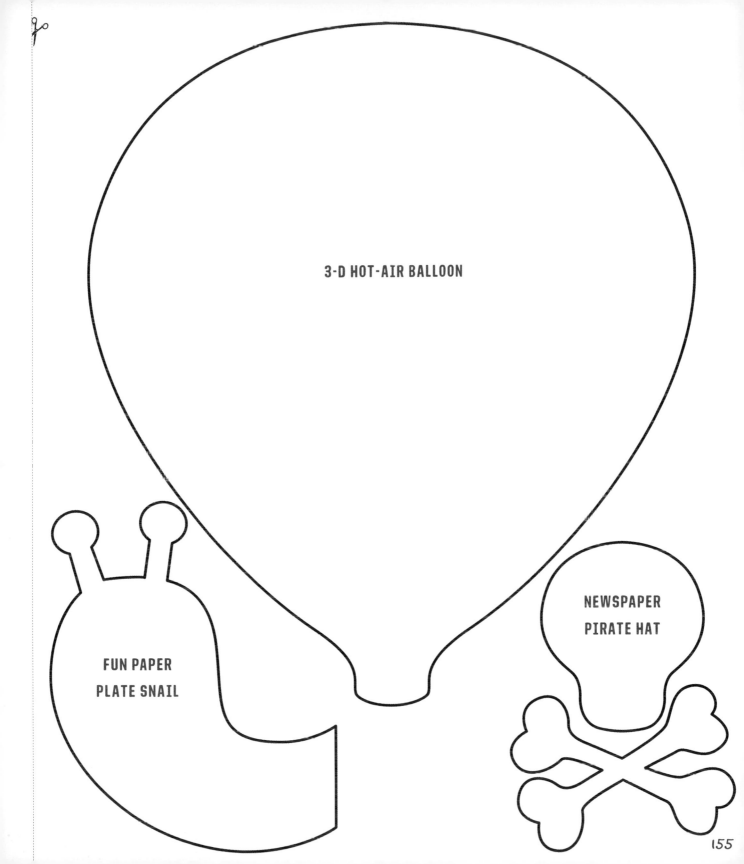

3-D HOT-AIR BALLOON

FUN PAPER
PLATE SNAIL

NEWSPAPER
PIRATE HAT

INDEX

A

adult assistance required
3-D Hot-Air Balloon, 46–47
Awesome Cardboard Castle, 91–93
Build Your Own Marble Maze, 78–79
Cereal Box Farm Puppet Theater, 88–90
Colorful Easter Basket, 116–117
Cool Superhero Mask, 96–97
Crystal Growing Project, 54–55
Magnet Frame, 114–115
Margarine Container Birthday Cake, 142–143
Mason Jar Spring Globe, 120–121
Milk Carton Bird Feeder, 134–135
Pouch Bottle Cap Flower, 138–139
Rainbow Bottle Cap Paint Palette, 140–141
Rainbow Turtle Puzzle, 74–75
Shoebox Aquarium, 84–85
Silly Tissue Box Monster, 80–81
Simple Princess Crown, 94–95
Simple Sailboat, 102–103
Supply Organizer, 30–31

B

baby food jars
Silly Face Jars, 128–129
Smell Jar Game, 122–123
beads: Homemade Kaleidoscope, 34–37
beans: Bottle Maracas, 130–131
birds: Mason Jar Spring Globe, 120–121
birdseed: Milk Carton Bird Feeder, 134–135
borax: Crystal Growing Project, 54–55
bottle caps
Bottle Cap Bees, 136–137
Build Your Own Marble Maze, 78–79
Pouch Bottle Cap Flower, 138–139
Rainbow Bottle Cap Paint Palette, 140–141
bowls: Spring Discovery Bottle, 132–133

bubble wrap
Bottle Cap Bees, 136–137
Paper Roll Printing, 26–27
Rainbow Jellyfish, 82–83
Rainbow Turtle Puzzle, 74–75
Shoebox Aquarium, 84–85
butterflies
3-D Butterfly Bracelet, 18–19
Cheerful Butterfly, 14–15
Mason Jar Spring Globe, 120–121
buttons
Beautiful Flowers Card, 48–49
Cheerful Butterfly, 14–15
Cookie-Cutter Christmas Ornaments, 98–99
Easy Flower Stamps, 28–29
Fun Airplane, 104–105
Fun Snowman, 40–41
Indoor Mini-Garden, 50–51
Magnet Frame, 114–115
Milk Carton Bird Feeder, 134–135
Personalized Trinket Box, 112–113

C

candles (flameless): Tissue Paper Jar Luminaire, 126–127
canvas: Letter Initial Canvas Art, 62–63
cardboard
Adorable Torn-Paper Cactus, 64–65
Awesome Cardboard Castle, 91–93
Backyard Safari Binoculars, 24–25
Bottle Cap Bees, 136–137
Build Your Own Marble Maze, 78–79
Cereal Box Farm Puppet Theater, 88–90
Cookie-Cutter Christmas Ornaments, 98–99
Cool Superhero Mask, 96–97
Cute Owl, 12–13
Pouch Bottle Cap Flower, 138–139
Rainbow and Cloud with Pop Tabs, 76–77
Rainbow Bottle Cap Paint Palette, 140–141
Rainbow Jellyfish, 82–83
Rainbow Turtle Puzzle, 74–75
Shoebox Winter Diorama, 86–87
Simple Princess Crown, 94–95
Stacking Challenge, 32–33
Supply Organizer, 30–31

Three-Season Scrap Paper Trees, 60–61
cardstock
3-D Butterfly Bracelet, 18–19
3-D Hot-Air Balloon, 46–47
Adorable Torn-Paper Cactus, 64–65
Awesome Cardboard Castle, 91–93
Beautiful Flowers Card, 48–49
Bottle Cap Bees, 136–137
Cereal Box Farm Puppet Theater, 88–90
Cheerful Butterfly, 14–15
Cookie-Cutter Christmas Ornaments, 98–99
Cool Superhero Mask, 96–97
Cute Owl, 12–13
Easy Flower Stamps, 28–29
Easy Paper Fan, 106–107
Fun Paper Plate Snail, 58–59
Fun Snowman, 40–41
Homemade Kaleidoscope, 34–37
Indoor Mini-Garden, 50–51
Margarine Container Birthday Cake, 142–143
Newspaper Pirate Hat, 66–67
Newspaper Tropical Wreath, 70–71
Penguin Antarctica Play Scene, 42–43
Pouch Bottle Cap Flower, 138–139
Rainbow and Cloud with Pop Tabs, 76–77
Shoebox Aquarium, 84–85
Shoebox Winter Diorama, 86–87
Silly Tissue Box Monster, 80–81
Simple Sailboat, 102–103
Thankful Turkey, 16–17
Three-Season Scrap Paper Trees, 60–61
cereal boxes
Cereal Box Farm Puppet Theater, 88–90
Cool Superhero Mask, 96–97
clothespins
Fun Airplane, 104–105
Magnet Frame, 114–115
construction paper
Cheerful Butterfly, 14–15
Fun Paper Plate Snail, 58–59
Fun Snowman, 40–41
Penguin Antarctica Play Scene, 42–43

Pouch Bottle Cap Flower, 138–139
Thankful Turkey, 16–17
cookie cutters
    Cookie-Cutter Christmas
        Ornaments, 98–99
    Plastic Container Suncatcher,
        144–145
cotton balls
    Penguin Antarctica Play Scene,
        42–43
    Rainbow and Cloud with Pop
        Tabs, 76–77
    Shoebox Winter Diorama, 86–87
cotton swabs: Shoebox Winter
    Diorama, 86–87
craft gems
    3-D Butterfly Bracelet, 18–19
    Magnet Frame, 114–115
    Personalized Trinket Box, 112–113
    Simple Princess Crown, 94–95
    Sparkly Necklace, 20–21
craft sticks
    Cereal Box Farm Puppet Theater,
        88–90
    Fun Airplane, 104–105
    Simple Sailboat, 102–103

D
dowels
    Milk Carton Bird Feeder, 134–135
    Pouch Bottle Cap Flower, 138–139

E
egg cartons
    3-D Hot-Air Balloon, 46–47
    Beautiful Flowers Card, 48–49
    Crystal Growing Project, 54–55
    Fun Snowman, 40–41
    Indoor Mini-Garden, 50–51
    Penguin Antarctica Play Scene,
        42–43
    Rainbow Caterpillar, 44–45
    Seed Starter Planters, 52–53
elastic
    Cool Superhero Mask, 96–97
    Simple Princess Crown, 94–95

F
felt: Cookie-Cutter Christmas
    Ornaments, 98–99
fishing line
    Rainbow and Cloud with Pop
        Tabs, 76–77
    Shoebox Aquarium, 84–85

flowers
    Beautiful Flowers Card, 48–49
    Easy Flower Stamps, 28–29
    Indoor Mini-Garden, 50–51
    Mason Jar Spring Globe, 120–121
    Newspaper Tropical Wreath,
        70–71
    Personalized Trinket Box, 112–113
    Pouch Bottle Cap Flower, 138–139
    Silly Face Jars, 128–129
    Spring Discovery Bottle, 132–133
foam shapes: Paper Roll Printing,
    26–27
foil board sheet: Homemade
    Kaleidoscope, 34–37
food coloring: Crystal Growing
    Project, 54–55
funnels: Spring Discovery Bottle,
    132–133

G
googly eyes
    Bottle Cap Bees, 136–137
    Cereal Box Farm Puppet Theater,
        88–90
    Cheerful Butterfly, 14–15
    Fun Paper Plate Snail, 58–59
    Penguin Antarctica Play Scene,
        42–43
    Rainbow and Cloud with Pop
        Tabs, 76–77
    Rainbow Caterpillar, 44–45
    Rainbow Jellyfish, 82–83
    Shoebox Aquarium, 84–85
    Silly Face Jars, 128–129
    Silly Tissue Box Monster, 80–81
    Thankful Turkey, 16–17

H
hot glue gun
    3-D Hot-Air Balloon, 46–47
    Awesome Cardboard Castle,
        91–93
    Build Your Own Marble Maze,
        78–79
    Colorful Easter Basket, 116–117
    Cool Superhero Mask, 96–97
    Magnet Frame, 114–115
    Margarine Container Birthday
        Cake, 142–143
    Mason Jar Spring Globe, 120–121
    Milk Carton Bird Feeder, 134–135
    Pouch Bottle Cap Flower, 138–139

Rainbow Bottle Cap Paint Palette,
    140–141
Shoebox Aquarium, 84–85
Simple Princess Crown, 94–95
Simple Sailboat, 102–103
Supply Organizer, 30–31

I
ice pop sticks
    Boredom Buster Jar, 110–111
    Build Your Own Marble Maze,
        78–79
    Cereal Box Farm Puppet Theater,
        88–90
    Colorful Easter Basket, 116–117
    Easy Paper Fan, 106–107
    Fun Airplane, 104–105
    Indoor Mini-Garden, 50–51
    Magnet Frame, 114–115
    Milk Carton Bird Feeder, 134–135
    Personalized Trinket Box, 112–113
    Silly Tissue Box Monster, 80–81
    Simple Sailboat, 102–103
    Weather Puzzle, 108–109

J
jars
    Boredom Buster Jar, 110–111
    Crystal Growing Project, 54–55
    Dinosaur Terrarium, 124–125
    Mason Jar Spring Globe, 120–121
    Pouch Bottle Cap Flower, 138–139
    Rainbow Jellyfish, 82–83
    Silly Face Jars, 128–129
    Smell Jar Game, 122–123
    Tissue Paper Jar Luminaire,
        126–127
juice cartons: Milk Carton Bird
    Feeder, 134–135

M
magazines: Three Season Scrap
    Paper Trees, 60–61
magnets: Magnet Frame, 114–115
magnifying glasses: Crystal
    Growing Project, 54–55
marbles: Build Your Own Marble
    Maze, 78–79
margarine containers: Margarine
    Container Birthday Cake,
    142–143
markers
    3-D Butterfly Bracelet, 18–19

Adorable Torn-Paper Cactus, 64–65
Boredom Buster Jar, 110–111
Bottle Cap Bees, 136–137
Build Your Own Marble Maze, 78–79
Cereal Box Farm Puppet Theater, 88–90
Cheerful Butterfly, 14–15
Cookie-Cutter Christmas Ornaments, 98–99
Cute Owl, 12–13
Easy Monkey Face, 68–69
Fun Paper Plate Snail, 58–59
Fun Snowman, 40–41
Homemade Kaleidoscope, 34–37
Plastic Container Suncatcher, 144–145
Rainbow Caterpillar, 44–45
Rainbow Jellyfish, 82–83
Shoebox Aquarium, 84–85
Silly Face Jars, 128–129
Silly Tissue Box Monster, 80–81
Thankful Turkey, 16–17
Weather Puzzle, 108–109
Mason jars
Crystal Growing Project, 54–55
Mason Jar Spring Globe, 120–121
Pouch Bottle Cap Flower, 138–139
Tissue Paper Jar Luminaire, 126–127
milk cartons
Milk Carton Bird Feeder, 134–135
Rainbow and Cloud with Pop Tabs, 76–77
Rainbow Bottle Cap Paint Palette, 140–141
moss
Dinosaur Terrarium, 124–125
Mason Jar Spring Globe, 120–121

N

newspaper
Cute Owl, 12–13
Easy Monkey Face, 68–69
Newspaper Pirate Hat, 66–67
Newspaper Tropical Wreath, 70–71

P

packaging foam: Penguin Antarctica Play Scene, 42–43

paints
3-D Butterfly Bracelet, 18–19
3-D Hot-Air Balloon, 46–47
Adorable Torn-Paper Cactus, 64–65
Awesome Cardboard Castle, 91–93
Backyard Safari Binoculars, 24–25
Beautiful Flowers Card, 48–49
Boredom Buster Jar, 110–111
Bottle Cap Bees, 136–137
Bottle Maracas, 130–131
Build Your Own Marble Maze, 78–79
Cereal Box Farm Puppet Theater, 88–90
Cheerful Butterfly, 14–15
Colorful Easter Basket, 116–117
Cookie-Cutter Christmas Ornaments, 98–99
Cool Superhero Mask, 96–97
Cute Owl, 12–13
Easy Flower Stamps, 28–29
Easy Monkey Face, 68–69
Easy Paper Fan, 106–107
Fun Airplane, 104–105
Fun Snowman, 40–41
Homemade Kaleidoscope, 34–37
Indoor Mini-Garden, 50–51
Letter Initial Canvas Art, 62–63
Magnet Frame, 114–115
Margarine Container Birthday Cake, 142–143
Milk Carton Bird Feeder, 134–135
Newspaper Pirate Hat, 66–67
Newspaper Tropical Wreath, 70–71
Paper Roll Printing, 26–27
Penguin Antarctica Play Scene, 42–43
Personalized Trinket Box, 112–113
Pouch Bottle Cap Flower, 138–139
Rainbow and Cloud with Pop Tabs, 76–77
Rainbow Bottle Cap Paint Palette, 140–141
Rainbow Caterpillar, 44–45
Rainbow Jellyfish, 82–83
Rainbow Rainstick, 22–23
Rainbow Turtle Puzzle, 74–75
Shoebox Aquarium, 84–85
Shoebox Winter Diorama, 86–87
Silly Face Jars, 128–129
Silly Tissue Box Monster, 80–81

Simple Princess Crown, 94–95
Simple Sailboat, 102–103
Smell Jar Game, 122–123
Sparkly Necklace, 20–21
Spring Discovery Bottle, 132–133
Stacking Challenge, 32–33
Supply Organizer, 30–31
Thankful Turkey, 16–17
Weather Puzzle, 108–109
paper bags
Rainbow Rainstick, 22–23
Smell Jar Game, 122–123
paper plates
Easy Flower Stamps, 28–29
Fun Paper Plate Snail, 58–59
Newspaper Tropical Wreath, 70–71
Rainbow Jellyfish, 82–83
paper rolls
3-D Butterfly Bracelet, 18–19
Awesome Cardboard Castle, 91–93
Backyard Safari Binoculars, 24–25
Build Your Own Marble Maze, 78–79
Cheerful Butterfly, 14–15
Cute Owl, 12–13
Easy Flower Stamps, 28–29
Homemade Kaleidoscope, 34–37
Paper Roll Printing, 26–27
Rainbow Rainstick, 22–23
Sparkly Necklace, 20–21
Stacking Challenge, 32–33
Supply Organizer, 30–31
Thankful Turkey, 16–17
pebbles: Dinosaur Terrarium, 124–125
pencils
3-D Hot-Air Balloon, 46–47
Adorable Torn-Paper Cactus, 64–65
Bottle Cap Bees, 136–137
Cereal Box Farm Puppet Theater, 88–90
Cookie-Cutter Christmas Ornaments, 98–99
Cool Superhero Mask, 96–97
Easy Monkey Face, 68–69
Fun Paper Plate Snail, 58–59
Indoor Mini-Garden, 50–51
Letter Initial Canvas Art, 62–63
Milk Carton Bird Feeder, 134–135
Newspaper Pirate Hat, 66–67

Newspaper Tropical Wreath, 70–71
Pouch Bottle Cap Flower, 138–139
Rainbow and Cloud with Pop Tabs, 76–77
Rainbow Caterpillar, 44–45
Rainbow Jellyfish, 82–83
Rainbow Turtle Puzzle, 74–75
Shoebox Winter Diorama, 86–87
Simple Princess Crown, 94–95
Smell Jar Game, 122–123
Weather Puzzle, 108–109
petal template: Newspaper Tropical Wreath, 70–71
pipe cleaners
Beautiful Flowers Card, 48–49
Cheerful Butterfly, 14–15
Easy Flower Stamps, 28–29
Fun Snowman, 40–41
Penguin Antarctica Play Scene, 42–43
Rainbow Caterpillar, 44–45
Shoebox Aquarium, 84–85
plants
Dinosaur Terrarium, 124–125
Seed Starter Planters, 52–53
Silly Face Jars, 128–129
plastic bottles
Bottle Maracas, 130–131
Spring Discovery Bottle, 132–133
plastic containers
Homemade Kaleidoscope, 34–35
Margarine Container Birthday Cake, 142–143
Plastic Container Suncatcher, 144–145
Seed Starter Planters, 52–53
pom-poms
Cheerful Butterfly, 14–15
Cookie-Cutter Christmas Ornaments, 98–99
Fun Airplane, 104–105
Fun Snowman, 40–41
Magnet Frame, 114–115
Margarine Container Birthday Cake, 142–143
Penguin Antarctica Play Scene, 42–43
Silly Tissue Box Monster, 80–81
pop tabs: Rainbow and Cloud with Pop Tabs, 76–77
potting soil: Seed Starter Planters, 52–53

R
ribbon
Beautiful Flowers Card, 48–49
Newspaper Tropical Wreath, 70–71
rice
Rainbow Rainstick, 22–23
Spring Discovery Bottle, 132–133
rocks
Dinosaur Terrarium, 124–125
Silly Face Jars, 128–129
rubber bands
Easy Flower Stamps, 28–29
Rainbow Rainstick, 22–23
Smell Jar Game, 122–123

S
safety, 9
seeds
Milk Carton Bird Feeder, 134–135
Seed Starter Planters, 52–53
shoeboxes
Shoebox Aquarium, 84–85
Shoebox Winter Diorama, 86–87
soil
Dinosaur Terrarium, 124–125
Seed Starter Planters, 52–53
stickers
Cookie-Cutter Christmas Ornaments, 98–99
Cool Superhero Mask, 96–97
Homemade Kaleidoscope, 34–37
Rainbow Rainstick, 22–23
sticks: Mason Jar Spring Globe, 120–121
stones
Mason Jar Spring Globe, 120–121
Spring Discovery Bottle, 132–133
string
Backyard Safari Binoculars, 24–25
Magnet Frame, 114–115
Plastic Container Suncatcher, 144–145
Rainbow and Cloud with Pop Tabs, 76–77
Rainbow Jellyfish, 82–83
Shoebox Aquarium, 84–85

T
templates
butterfly, 18–19, 151
butterfly wing, 14–15, 151
fish, 84–85, 153
fox, 86–87, 149

hot-air balloon, 46–47, 155
mini-garden, 50–51, 151
monkey face, 68–69, 153
petal, 70–71, 149
polar bear, 86–87, 149
skull and crossbones, 66–67, 155
snail, 58–59, 155
superhero mask, 96–97, 151
tree, 86–87, 149
turkey feather, 16–17, 151
tissue boxes: Silly Tissue Box Monster, 80–81
tissue paper
Adorable Torn-Paper Cactus, 64–65
Margarine Container Birthday Cake, 142–143
Newspaper Tropical Wreath, 70–71
Plastic Container Suncatcher, 144–145
Tissue Paper Jar Luminaire, 126–127
toothpicks: Awesome Cardboard Castle, 91–93
toys
Dinosaur Terrarium, 124–125
Spring Discovery Bottle, 132–133
twine
3-D Hot-Air Balloon, 46–47
Backyard Safari Binoculars, 24–25
Cookie-Cutter Christmas Ornaments, 98–99
Milk Carton Bird Feeder, 134–135
Rainbow and Cloud with Pop Tabs, 76–77

W
washi tape
Backyard Safari Binoculars, 24–25
Rainbow Rainstick, 22–23
water
Crystal Growing Project, 54–55
Seed Starter Planters, 52–53
wax paper: Spring Discovery Bottle, 132–133

Y
yarn
Backyard Safari Binoculars, 24–25
Cookie-Cutter Christmas Ornaments, 98–99